Eat, Drink, Think

Also available from Bloomsbury

The Emergence of National Food, edited by Atsuko Ichijo,
Venetia Johannes, and Ronald Ranta
Introducing the Sociology of Food and Eating, Anne Murcott
Taste, Politics, and Identities in Mexican Food,
edited by Steffan Igor Ayora-Diaz

Eat, Drink, Think

*What Ancient Greece Can Tell Us about
Food and Wine*

David Roochnik

BLOOMSBURY ACADEMIC
LONDON · NEW YORK · OXFORD · NEW DELHI · SYDNEY

BLOOMSBURY ACADEMIC
Bloomsbury Publishing Plc
50 Bedford Square, London, WC1B 3DP, UK
1385 Broadway, New York, NY 10018, USA

BLOOMSBURY, BLOOMSBURY ACADEMIC and the Diana logo are trademarks of
Bloomsbury Publishing Plc

First published in Great Britain 2020

A catalogue record for this book is available from the British Library.

A catalog record for this book is available from the Library of Congress.

ISBN: HB: 978-1-3501-2076-1
PB: 978-1-3501-2077-8
ePDF: 978-1-3501-2078-5
ePub: 978-1-3501-2079-2

Typeset by Newgen KnowledgeWorks Pvt. Ltd., Chennai, India
Printed and bound in Great Britain

To find out more about our authors and books visit www.bloomsbury.com
and sign up for our newsletters.

Dedicated to Gina, Alfredo, and Alessandra,
who taught me to eat well.

Come, we'll shake off this mourning mood of ours and think of supper.
—Homer, *Odyssey* IV.229

Surely you don't think that a philosopher cares much about such so-called pleasures as those of food and drink?
—Plato, *Phaedo*, 64d

Contents

Copyright Acknowledgements   ix
Prelude   x

1   The Eatingest Epic   1
        I Supper in the *Odyssey*   1
       II A Good Meal as an Affirmation of Transience   3
      III Helen's Opiate   9
       IV The Vital Importance of Stories   10
        V The *Odyssey* as a Story about a Storyteller   12
       VI Identity and Names   20
      VII Recognitions   22
     VIII The Shades in Hades   28
       IX Justice in the *Odyssey*   30
        X The *Odyssey* as an Affirmation of Life   35

Interlude[1]   37

2   Dionysus   45
        I Euripides' *Bacchae*   45
       II The Dionysian Journey of Lawrence Osborne   58
      III William James as a Dionysian   61
       IV Nietzsche's *The Birth of Tragedy*   66

Interlude[2]   75

3   Socrates   79
        I The *Symposium*   79
       II Socrates' Metaphorical Feast   86
      III Recollection in Plato's *Phaedo*   90
       IV Christianity: Spiritual Nourishment   94
        V Homer's Nightmare: Soylent   100

Interlude³   105

4   Aristotle   117
      I The Four Issues of This Book   117
     II Aristotle as Zoologist   120
    III Form as Species   121
    IV Aristotle as Apollinian   124
     V The Nutritive *Psuchê*   127
    VI The Perceptive *Psuchê*   133
   VII The Generation of Animals   137
  VIII Aristotle's Intellect   138
    IX Is the *Psuchê* Immortal?   143
     X What Is Knowing?   146
    XI The Fractured *Psuchê*   150

Postlude   153

Notes   163
Bibliography   167
Index   169

Copyright Acknowledgements

The author is grateful to the following sources for permission to reproduce in this book material previously published elsewhere:

Excerpts from THE ODYSSEY by Homer, translated by Robert Fitzgerald. Copyright © 1961, 1963 by Robert Fitzgerald. Copy renewed 1989 by Benedict R. C. Fitzgerald, on behalf of the Fitzgerald children. Reprinted by permission of Farrar, Straus and Giroux.

Excerpts from THE BACCHAE by Euripides, translated by William Arrowsmith. Copyright © 1959 by the University of Chicago. Published 1959. Paperback edition 1968. Reprinted by permission of the University of Chicago Press.

Prelude

(1)

The food, as usual in my home, is simple and lovely. Fresh scallops bought from Cindy, a woman who goes to the docks every day, and then sells her goods at a local store in Coolidge Corner. Fresh asparagus from the farmers' market at Copley Square. It's spring in Boston, they're in season, and we'll be eating them every day until they disappear from the stalls. I marinate both in olive oil and then throw them on a hot grill. While they're cooking, and it doesn't take long, I finish up the pasta. In the pan, some cherry tomatoes (industrial), lots of garlic, and tiny flakes of dried habanero chilies, just enough to add an almost imperceptible sting, sizzle in oil. I throw in a modest pat of butter. When the spaghetti is almost done, I take it out of the boiling water, drain it vigorously, and dump it into the pan, where I mix it thoroughly in the sauce. Then I sprinkle with finishing oil, a really nice one from Tuscany. Outlandishly expensive, but the large bottle will last for months. The hot pan goes to the table for serving, and then the scallops and asparagus, both browned nicely, come to the plates. A warm evening, we're sitting on our deck, chilled white wine in our glasses. I pause for the briefest moment. Then, imitating my Italian friends, I say "buon appetito" to Gina, who returns the greeting, and only then do we begin to eat. A bite of scallop comes first. It's rich, succulent, sweet.

And then, as almost always, especially at home, and especially when it's just me and Gina, I eat too fast. Having taken a long swim earlier, I'm hungry. I wolf down the food. It all tastes wonderful. Oily and rich, strong flavors, rewarding texture. But I can't slow myself in order to savor it properly, to give this good food the attention it deserves. (Gina can.) Instead, big loads on the fork rapidly follow one after the other. I used to reprimand myself for eating so fast, but I've long realized this is pointless. I'm gripped by a fervor I do not understand and cannot suppress. All the more puzzling since after supper there is nowhere I have to go, nothing I have to do. And no Cossacks are banging on the door. At least not yet.

My plate is soon empty. All that remains in the pan is oily residue, and this I lap up with a chunk of a baguette purchased a few hours earlier at Clear Flour, the superb little bakery a few blocks from my house.

With the table cleared, and the dishes washed, gelato comes out of the freezer. Made in Maine, titled "Fiasco," and purchased at a high-end supermarket, it's as close to the real Italian thing we know. Smooth, rich dark chocolate, spiked with sea-salted caramel. Expensive, but we don't eat too much. We don't even bother putting it into bowls. Instead, we each take a few turns with our spoons.

It's still warm, and so we take a walk. To the same supermarket where we bought the gelato. We restock our supply. I put an ice pack in my backpack to keep our stash cold.

We're done, we're home, and the night has barely begun. Soon I'll be watching the Red Sox or the Celtics on TV. The sound will be turned off and I'll pay little attention. Then I will struggle, as usual, with sleep. I'll toss and turn and vibrate, get out of bed, walk around the house, and eat whatever I can find: what's left of the baguette, some crackers and jam, yogurt, and maple syrup. Two or three times a night I repeat this pattern.

When morning finally arrives, I will wash away the vestiges of troublesome night with a cold shower, quickly eat some toast while reading the sports page, and head to my office. After coffee and a few puffs of a cigarette, after zipping through emails, scanning box scores, and glancing at the news to see if anything has blown up, I will settle down to write. For the next several hours, I'll be at my desk. But never for long. I'll jump out of my chair every few minutes. Another cigarette, short hikes to the bathroom, pour more coffee, tidy up my desk, open the window, quick peeks at email, the *New York Times*, and the Red Sox, stand up to stretch, clip my fingernails, reheat the coffee, grab a handful of trail mix, close the window. Still, gripped by a force I do not understand, I will stubbornly return to the keyboard, trying to eke out a concentrated thought, a well-crafted sentence or two that might … that might what? Matter?

When I take a few puffs of my morning cigarette, the necessary jump start of my day, I imagine my afternoon exercise in the gym, when I will breathe hard for an hour or so, and clean out the crap in my lungs. I will swim, a crummy stroke, looking ahead, trying to stay afloat. Then I'll sit in the hot tub before I shower to clean the rest of me. Dirty and clean, empty and full, crappy and not too bad, and the cycle keeps on spinning till the sun goes down.

What kind of life is this, anyway?

1

The Eatingest Epic

I Supper in the *Odyssey*

Come, we'll shake off this mourning mood of ours
  and think of supper.

Homer, Odyssey IV.229[1]

The lines above, also used as the first epigraph of this book, are spoken by Meneláos in Homer's *Odyssey*. He is at home, hosting a wedding feast for both his children, when he is informed that strangers have arrived at his doorstep. His friend Eteóneus is unsure whether to invite them to join the party. Meneláos rebukes him sharply:

> You were no idiot before, Eteóneus,
> but here you are talking like a child of ten.
> Could we have made it home again—and Zeus
> give us no more hard roving!—if other men
> had never fed us, given us lodging?
> Bring these men to be our guests; unhitch their teams!

IV.33–9

In the world of the *Odyssey*, "strangers and beggars/ come from Zeus" (VI.221) and so merit special consideration. As such, being a good host and welcoming them—and, above all, this means offering food and drink—is a cardinal imperative. And so Meneláos, good man that he is, warmly invites the strangers in, and treats them royally:

> Maidservants gave them baths, anointed them,
> held out fresh tunics, cloaked them warm; and soon
> they took tall thrones beside the son of Atreus.
> Here a maid tipped out water for their hands

from a golden pitcher into a silver bowl,
and set a polished table near at hand;
the larder mistress with her tray of loaves
and savories came, dispensing all her best,
and the carver heaped their platters high
with various meats, and put down cups of gold.

IV.53–63

Details lovingly saturate this scene. The strangers, ragged from hard travels, are given warm clothes and a bowl of water in which to wash their hands. But not just any bowl: it's a silver one, and the water is poured from a golden pitcher. A table, freshly polished, is brought to them, and from it they are served ample portions of the best food in the house, including a variety of grilled meats. Finally, they are given cups made of gold to hold their wine. In Homer's *Odyssey*, the good host, the good person, spares nothing for his guests.

The guest code has its rules: Bathe and clothe strangers if they need it. Then feed them and give them something to drink. And only then ask for names. Meneláos does it right. "When you have supped," he tells his guests, "we hope to hear your names, forbears and families" (IV.67).

It turns out that these two strangers are, in fact, not so strange. Both are sons of Meneláos' old comrades from the war in Troy. One is Peisístratos, son of Nestor; the other is Telémakhos, son of Odysseus. They have come to Lakedaimon specifically to visit Meneláos since Telémakhos desperately wants information about his father, who has been gone for twenty years, and whom he has never met.

After they introduce themselves, the men share stories. And that's when the gloom sets in. The Trojan War was a ten-year ordeal of terrible violence, in which good men on both sides, including Peisístratos' brother, were killed. Furthermore, since travel in the ancient world was no easy matter, even after the war had ended with the Greeks as victors, their voyage home was a prolonged struggle. Odysseus had not yet returned, and Meneláos himself spent years wandering before he made it back to Greece. When he finally did, he discovered that his brother, Agamemnon, had been murdered by his own wife and her lover. Despair threatens to overwhelm him:

How gladly I should live one third as rich
to have my friends back safe at home!—my friends
who died on Troy's wide seaboard, far
from the grazing lands of Argos.

But as things are, nothing but grief is left me
for those companions.

IV.105–110

The feast seems to be on the verge of emotional collapse as "a twinging ache of grief rose up in everyone" (IV.195). The men, all of whom feel the pain of irretrievable loss, begin to weep. But then Meneláos catches himself and utters the lines with which this chapter opened. Let's eat, he says. Since a Homeric supper is never without wine, he calls his guests to the table not only to share a meal but also to take the edge off with drink.

Meneláos' response is quintessentially Homeric, for the *Odyssey* is, to cite a wonderful phrase attributed to Henry Fielding, "the eatingest epic." This chapter will be devoted to explaining what this means and why it is worth thinking about.

II A Good Meal as an Affirmation of Transience

In the poet's eyes, loss defines human life. If death by disease, accident, or violence manages to be avoided, the best-case scenario for each of us is to grow old, wither, and then disappear. For Homer's is a world in which nothing is permanent or entirely solid. One story, told by Meneláos, vividly expresses this view.

After departing from Troy, his ship was becalmed on an island near Egypt where there was no wind to power its sails. Provisions were running low, and Meneláos and his men were failing. Fortunately, he bumped into a goddess who took pity on him: Eidothea, daughter of Proteus, the old man of the sea. Meneláos begs her for help. How, he asks her, "am I going to make my voyage home?" (IV.409). She tells him that he must find her father, for only he knows the route back to Greece. But this is no easy task. For Proteus is, well, Protean. He is a shape-shifter who "can take the forms/ of all the beasts, and water, and blinding fire" (IV.446). Meneláos must therefore seize him and then somehow hold him fast. The moment to strike, Eidothea explains, is when, after having gathered his pet seals in a cave, Proteus takes a nap. Then Meneláos should grab him, and force him to stay still and to talk.

Meneláos follows Eidothea's directions carefully. He and a few of his men, draped in sealskins for disguise, catch Proteus when he is asleep:

When at last he slept
we gave a battlecry and plunged for him,
locking our hands behind him. But the old one's

tricks were not knocked out of him; far from it.
First he took on a whiskered lion's shape,
a serpent then; a leopard; a great boar;
then sousing water; then a tall green tree.
Still we hung on, by hook or crook, through everything,
until the Ancient saw defeat and grimly
opened his lips.

IV.483–92

This story is the keynote of Homer's *Odyssey*. The world itself is Protean. It has no stable shape, no abiding form. Instead, it is fluid, ever shifting, on the move. Human beings, however, need some measure of stability in order to survive. Meneláos, for one, wants to go home, and for this he needs a reliable path to follow. But to acquire it he must use violence. He must hold Proteus down and force him to provide information. For the world does not give us form for free. It must be won by hard human effort, and the victory will never be more than brief.

Dwell, for a moment, on the word "form." Its Greek version is *eidos*, which is derived from the verb "to see." In its most basic meaning, then, an *eidos* is the "look" of a thing. And it is precisely such "looks" that make the world in which we live intelligible.

You enter a classroom and, almost instantaneously, see a variety of objects: other people, desks, tables, windows, books, carpet on the floor. But you have no doubt as to where you will sit: in one of the chairs. These you recognize, again almost immediately. And so you select an empty one and seat yourself. Rarely will you make a mistake in this exercise. You will not sit on a table. No, you will find a properly empty chair and, unless it is broken, it will accommodate your body when you plunk yourself down.

You successfully navigated the multitude of objects in the classroom and found your seat for a simple reason. A chair looks like a chair and not a table. Now, there may be many chairs in the room. Some may be black and made of wood, others brown and made of plastic. But this diversity does not thwart your effort to find a place to sit. For, however much they vary, they are all alike in one decisive respect: they look like chairs. This is hardly surprising since they have been built specifically to accomplish the same one task, which is to allow a human body to sit in them. Their form follows their function.

The vast variety of different chairs in the world come and go. But the form of the chair is (relatively) stable, which is why you recognize one when you see it. Turn off the lights in the classroom, however, and the story changes. You would not know where to sit. Yes, of course, by feeling your way around the room you would eventually locate an empty chair by tracing objects with your hands. But this would take a while. Most of us, most of the time, perform such an operation without noticeable effort. We see what looks like an empty chair and then sit in it. The fact that chairs share a form is why, even if you were entering the classroom for the first time, you were not terribly confused. The room made sense to you. Despite its many unique features, it was not hugely different from the classrooms you have entered in the past.

Were there no forms in the world, our lives would not make a bit of sense. But the world does make sense to us, at least most of the time (especially during the day), and so there must be forms. The question is, where do they come from? What is the source of the stability in our experience that renders it intelligible? For Homer, the answer is forceful human effort. His world is Protean, shape-shifting, fluid, and so is tokened best by water rather than stone. Just as Meneláos must extract the information he needs from Proteus by subduing him with violence, so too must we work hard to impose form, even if all too briefly, on the world.

Homer smuggles in a nice little joke in his telling of this story. Proteus' daughter is **Eido**thea, which in Greek means "divine form." Precisely because it is stable and (relatively) permanent, form is "divine." But humans are not. Meneláos himself makes this point, one absolutely central to the *Odyssey*, when he rebukes Telémakhos, who, upon entering the grand hall of the palace, says the following to his companion Peisístratos:

"My dear friend, can you believe your eyes?—
the murmuring hall, how luminous it is
with bronze, gold, amber, silver and ivory!
This is the way the court of Zeus must be,
inside, upon Olympos. What a wonder!"

But splendid Meneláos had overheard him
and spoke out on the instant to them both:

"Young friends, no mortal man can vie with Zeus.
His home and all his treasure are for ever"

IV. 75–85

Meneláos, clearly functioning as a surrogate father to Telémakhos, is teaching the boy a fundamental lesson: "No mortal man can vie with Zeus." Homeric (Olympian) gods are forever. They are born and then mature, but they neither get old nor die, and so their glorious forms never degrade. Ours, however, do. And that they do, a fact of which we are irremediably conscious, is the defining feature of our lives. The gods of the *Odyssey* are thus radical foils. Through their contrast, they make apparent what is essential about being human: we are passing away in continual, even if gradual, deformation; they are not. For this reason, the worst mistake human beings can make is to think themselves a god.

A bit later in the *Odyssey*, Homer expresses this same point with astonishing clarity. We learn that Odysseus has been living on an island with the divine nymph Kalypso, who adores him. But despite her unfailing beauty he is anything but happy.

> The sweet days of his life time
> were running out in anguish over his exile,
> for long ago the nymph had ceased to please.
> Though he fought shy of her and her desire,
> he lay with her each night, for she compelled him
>
> V.162

He had become the nymph's sex slave, and despite the pleasures of her bed he is tiring of their time together. Kalypso is baffled that this should be so. After all, she says,

> I fed him, loved him, sang that he should not die
> nor grow old, ever, in all the days to come.
>
> V. 144

Kalypso had offered Odysseus immortality and never-ending youth—to make him a god. But Odysseus, appreciative of his own humanity, declined her invitation. He wants to go home to his wife Penelope, who is as mortal as he. Fearing Kalypso will be angry with him, he explains why:

> My lady goddess, here is no cause for anger.
> My quiet Penelope—how well I know—
> would seem a shade before your majesty,
> death and old age being unknown to you,
> while she must die. Yet, it is true, each day
> I long for home, long for the sight of home
>
> V.225

The hero of the *Odyssey* prefers deterioration and death to immortal life, bread and wine to nectar and ambrosia. In short, Odysseus says yes to transience. He avows the goodness of time's passing and the inevitable loss of form and all we hold dear. Little wonder, then, that the very first word (in Greek) of the *Odyssey* is "man."

There is no better way to acknowledge the relentless flow of time, and to affirm its goodness, than by celebrating the act of eating. For food is the very embodiment of the transient. It must be consumed in order for it to be what it is and to do its job. Only when it enters the mouth and then is digested, only when it has disappeared, does it supply the energy the body needs in order to maintain its form, however briefly it may do so. And shortly after eating, the body needs to be replenished. Filling and emptying, refilling and emptying again: such is the cycle of our days. On and on this repetitive sequence goes, for as long as an organism has the energy to keep itself alive.

A splendid, well-presented meal, with wine served in golden cups, may seem to be a small work of art. But unlike the marble sculpture in the museum, whose presence seems to boast of its permanence, the carefully arranged food on the plate is designed to be eaten, to pass away. To say yes to it is to do precisely what Odysseus did with Kalypso: say yes to mortality. The next time, then, that you sit down to a fine meal, served on a lovely plate, pause for a moment before picking up your silver fork. Look at the food and say both thank-you and goodbye. In order to enjoy its taste, and to benefit from its nutrients, you must make it disappear. So too with our very lives.

Back to the *Odyssey:* Telémakhos has come to Lakedaimon to meet Meneláos. He needs help, for his home has been invaded by the "suitors." These are the young men of Ithaka who, during Odysseus' prolonged absence and presumed death, have occupied his household in the hope of winning the hand of his wife Penelope, and thereby gaining the riches of the lost hero.

> Now came the suitors,
> young bloods trooping in to their own seats
> on thrones or easy chairs. Attendants poured
> water over their fingers, while the maids
> piled baskets full of brown loaves near at hand,
> and houseboys brimmed the bowls with wine.
> Now they laid hands upon the ready feast
> and thought of nothing more.
>
> I.179–86

The suitors, like other bad guys in the *Odyssey*, eat badly. Uninvited, they nevertheless make themselves at home in Odysseus' palace. They order his servants to bring them food and drink, which they consume as if it were their own. They think only of wolfing down fine items from the ample larder. They are, by and large, arrogant louts taking advantage of Telémakhos' youth. Not surprisingly, the boy has no idea how to deal with them. They are older than he and there are over a hundred of them. Fortunately (like his father), he has the goddess Athena on his side. She comes to Ithaka in order to help him stand up for what is rightfully his. As she says,

> For my part, I shall visit Ithaka
> to put more courage in the son, and rouse him
> to call an assembly of the islanders,
> Akhaian gentlemen with flowing hair.
> He must warn off that wolf pack of the suitors
> who prey upon his flocks and dusky cattle.
>
> I.112–18

As she regularly does when she appears to mortals, Athena arrives in disguise. She claims to be Mentês, a sailor and longtime family friend. She reassures Telémakhos that "never in this world is Odysseus dead/ only detained somewhere in the wide sea" (I.240). But the boy is skeptical:

> Friend, let me put it in the plainest way.
> My mother says I am his son; I know not
> surely. Who has known his own engendering?
> I wish at least I had some happy man
> as father, growing old in his own house—
> but unknown death and silence are the fate
> of him that, since you ask, they call my father.
>
> I.258–64

Like most teenagers, Telémakhos is unsure of who he is. Even worse, bullied by the suitors and missing his father terribly, he is losing hope. "He's gone, no sign, no word of him; and I inherit/ trouble and tears" (I.288). He is on the verge of despair and wonders whether his pitiful fate is widely shared. "Who has known his own engendering?" he bleakly asks. Is there "nothing but grief" in this world?

Athena comes to Ithaka to make sure he does not succumb to the gloom threatening to overwhelm him. She is his mentor, determined to help him become an adult who knows how to occupy his proper place in the world— who knows how to struggle. For this reason she sends him on the journey to visit Meneláos.[2] Odysseus' old comrade will not only give Telémakhos the information he craves about his missing father, but he will function as a role model who can teach Telémakhos what it is to be a man.

III Helen's Opiate

To continue with the scene: After comparing stories, the men, recalling how much they have lost in the Trojan War and its aftermath, begin to weep. Meneláos snaps them out of their gloom by inviting them to the supper table. And then his wife, the all too beautiful Helen, whose abduction by the Trojan prince Paris sparked the war, takes over.

> The hero Meneláos' companion in arms,
> Asphalion, poured water for their hands,
> and once again they touched the food before them.
> But now it entered Helen's mind
> to drop into the wine that they were drinking
> an anodyne, mild magic of forgetfulness.
> Whoever drank this mixture in the wine bowl
> would be incapable of tears that day—
> though he should lose mother and father both,
> or see, with his own eyes, a son or brother
> mauled by weapons of bronze at his own gate.
>
> IV.232–33

The Greeks typically mixed their wine with water in a bowl before serving it. But Helen, eager to dispel the gloom enveloping the men, goes one step further. She spikes the drink with a powerful drug. She explains why:

> O Meneláos, Atreus' royal son,
> and you that are great heroes' sons, you know
> how Zeus gives all of us in turn
> good luck and bad luck, being all powerful.
>
> IV.252–56

The days of our lives continuously oscillate between good and bad, empty and full, and even the best of times soon fade into their opposite. Odysseus says much the same later in the book:

> Of mortal creatures, all that breathe and move,
> earth bears none frailer than mankind. What man

believes in woe to come, as long as valor
and tough knees are supplied him by the gods?
But when the gods in bliss bring miseries on
them will-nilly, blindly he endures.
Our minds are as the days are, dark or bright,
blown over by the father of gods and men.

XVIII.164–72

The brutally quick transition from gladness to woe, good luck to bad, today to tomorrow, is the essence of transience, and confronting it honestly can be paralyzing. Thus it is tempting, it may even seem reasonable, to succumb to just the sort of despair on whose edge both Meneláos and Telémakhos have teetered. Helen aims to ward this off, but she herself gives into another temptation: the oblivion of the opiate that she pours into the wine. No surprise, then, that soon after drinking from the bowl, Telémakhos wants to go to sleep. "Sweet sleep," he says, "will be a pleasure, drifting over us" (IV.318).

Opiated sleep may successfully distract, but it is no real salve, and it is Helen herself, a surprising woman, who suggests this. For she introduces another weapon to wield against despair:

So take refreshment, take your ease in hall,
and cheer the time with stories.

IV.255–6

Food, wine, and drugs are ways of coping with, ameliorating, or at least suppressing the suffering that attends the inevitability of loss. But storytelling is an even more powerful response to the human condition. This is the key lesson Telémakhos will learn from Meneláos and Helen. Supper with friends and strangers, replete with good food served on lovely plates and strong wine poured into cups of gold, can work its magic only if stories are exchanged.

IV The Vital Importance of Stories

A story—the Greek word is *muthos*, origin of our "myth"—has parts. In a good one, the chapters, scenes, or episodes fit together to form an organic unity in which each part contributes something to the whole. Aristotle defines a *muthos*, which for him means "plot" as well as "story," as "the arrangement of the incidents … it is complete and whole … it has a beginning, a middle and an end."[3] We need stories so acutely precisely because wholeness is what, in real life, is missing.

Recall an occasion on which you met someone new. You want to get to know her, and her to know you. For this you must exchange stories. What do you do? Where are you from? Where have you been, and where do you want to go next? If the conversation continues for a while, the two of you might want to learn about each other's families.

To get to know others is to hear their story. To get them to know you, you have to tell yours. Even more basically, to be able to recognize yourself, to have an identity you can bring to the table, you must be able to tell a story of yourself, to yourself.

To tell a life story, even a little one to exchange with someone you have just met, requires memory. The past must be connected to the present in order to explain why you are here now. For this reason, a person who has lost his memory—an old man, say, suffering from severe dementia—is finished. In the most concrete way, he is no longer himself. Memory by itself, however, cannot generate a story. For the present must be oriented to a future. You are here now because you desire, expect, and imagine to be somewhere else later. Only by being equipped with a story that has a beginning (past), middle (present), and end (future), and so is a unified package, or a whole, can a person gain a sense of being someone.

There is another reason why memory alone is insufficient to generate a little life story. Our minds are chock-full of details, almost all of which we count as irrelevant, or simply forget. If you were to ask me, "What did you do yesterday?" I could give you a long list of items. I wiped dust off a table. I poured hot coffee into a thermos and then brought it to my office. This is not what you, or I, want to hear. So I will tell you instead what transpired yesterday that I take to be worth mentioning. For this I must cull my memories and select only those that are salient in order to bring them to the fore. I had an enjoyable conversation with an intelligent and slightly mad woman. I'll tell you about her. But, of course, I won't simply repeat every word I can remember her saying. Instead, I'll mention (and paraphrase) the highlights in order to communicate the gist of the encounter. And I will arrange them into some kind of narrative order. If I don't do this, my telling will be no more than a transcript, and not a story at all. It will be both boring and unin*form*ative. For a story is not a list and so, above all else, a good one must have a unifying form or shape. So I will cut and paste my memories, round off the harsh edges, simplify or supplement when needed, bridge the gaps, and generate, as Aristotle puts it, an arrangement complete and whole. Regrettably, only a few people do this well.

In short, while memory is a necessary condition for the telling of a good story, it is hardly sufficient. In addition, the imagination must go to work, for it is the power we (somehow) deploy in order to transform a mass of memory items into a crafted whole, and to project ourselves to a future unknown. A story, then, even one as truthful as we can make it, is inevitably a "fiction," a word derived from the Latin *fingere*, "to form, fashion, make."

Stories, especially the little life stories we tell of ourselves, are fictions. For our experience is never actually complete and whole. Look within and, as if you were watching a movie, you will observe a ceaseless and jumpy flow of images, ideas, memories, fears, regrets, hopes, desires. We skip from past to future, neither of which is present now. Such is our transience, our awareness of the passage of time. And just as Meneláos must use force to stabilize Proteus, so too must we impose order upon the flux of our inner lives. To cope, we must make for ourselves a stable identity and a story to tell ourselves and others. We must generate a narrative, a sense of who we are. And in doing so, we fictionalize. This does not mean we intentionally deceive either others or ourselves. No, we fictionalize simply by telling a story with a beginning, a middle, and an end, by culling our storehouse of memories and then forming them into a unified narrative that directs the past toward an anticipated future. Even if I have changed considerably, I am, or so I must take myself to be, the same person who was here yesterday, and who imagines he will return tomorrow. This takes work.

See now the intimate link between stories and food. They both are needed to keep us intact, to maintain our form. Without them, we would disintegrate. No wonder they go so well together.

V The *Odyssey* as a Story about a Storyteller

Book V opens with Athena pleading with her father to release Odysseus from the sexual bondage imposed on him by Kalypso. Zeus heeds his favorite daughter, and so he sends Hermes, the messenger god, to visit the nymph, and to order her to release Odysseus. Kalypso not only complies—she really has no choice—but she even helps her beloved mortal build a ship. Odysseus then heads out to sea. But his trip doesn't last long. Soon Poseidon, who (for reasons to be explained shortly) hates Odysseus, sends a powerful storm, and the hero is shipwrecked. After two miserable days floundering in the water, he washes up on the island of Skerhía, where the Phaiákians live. Exhausted, he nonetheless manages to get himself ashore, where he promptly falls asleep in a pile of leaves. The next day the Phaiákian princess, Nausikaa, happens to be playing with some other girls close to where he sleeps. Their gleeful shouts awaken him. How he reacts, what he says and does, speaks volumes about who he is: the sweet-talker, the storyteller, par excellence.

> He pushed aside the bushes, breaking off
> with his great hand a single branch of olive,
> whose leaves might shield him in his nakedness;
> so came out rustling, like a mountain lion,
> rain-drenched, wind-buffeted, but in his might at ease,
>
> with burning eyes—who prowls among the herds
> or flocks, or after game, his hungry belly
> taking him near stout homesteads for his prey.
> Odysseus had this look, in his rough skin
> advancing on the girls with pretty braids;
> and he was driven on by hunger, too.
> Streaked with brine, and swollen, he terrified them,
> so that they fled, this way and that. Only
> Alkínoös' daughter stood her ground, being given
> a bold heart by Athena, and steady knees.
>
> She faced him, waiting. And Odysseus came,
> debating inwardly what he should do:
> embrace this beauty's knees in supplication?
> or stand apart, and, using honeyed speech,
> inquire the way to town, and beg some clothing?
> In his swift reckoning, he thought it best
> to trust in words.

VI.135–58

Odysseus leaves his hiding place in order to check out the girls. Staring at them, Homer writes, he is "like a mountain lion" whose "hungry belly" drives him to seek prey, whose eyes are "burning" as he "prowls among the herds." The simile suggests violence, and Odysseus is indeed on the prowl. But he has no intention of harming the girls. After all, he is in desperate need of their assistance. Instead, his fierce eyes are intensely examining the situation in order to figure out what to do next. Before he can decide, they spot him and, with the exception of Nausikaa, run away in fear. This is hardly surprising: they are young girls, and Odysseus is a large, filthy, naked man. He must then decide how best to approach Nausikaa. Should he kneel in front of her in supplication? On the one hand, that would be a proper way to treat a royal personage. On the other, he is naked. So he opts to speak to her from a distance. "Mistress, please," he says to her; "are you divine, or mortal?" (VI.161).

What a line! Odysseus, as usual, has scoped the situation perfectly and has figured out how to show both the utmost respect and to keep his distance. He continues: "Never," he says, "have I laid eyes on equal beauty/ in man or woman" (VI.171). This is surely untrue—after all, he has just left the embrace of the divine Kalypso—but it works. For such is the genius of Odysseus: he knows just what to say, and how to say it, to the right people at the right time. He is masterful in responding effectively to the specifics of an occasion. Unlike his heroic counterpart in the *Iliad*, Achilles, who is an unwavering man of blunt power, Odysseus is a hero of words and finesse. Above all else, he is flexible. He knows how to go with the flow.

Nausikaa is won over, and she, marvelous princess that she is, castigates the other girls for running away:

> This man is a castaway, poor fellow;
> we must take care of him. Strangers and beggars
> come from Zeus: a small gift, then, is friendly.
> Give our new guest some food and drink, and take him
> into the river, out of the wind, to bathe.
>
> VI.220–5

The girls "set out bread and wine before Odysseus,/ and ah! how ravenously that patient man/ took food and drink" (VI.265).

Next, Nausikaa takes him to the palace to meet her parents, the king and queen. They too prove to be exceptional hosts. After clothing and feeding him, letting him sleep, and entertaining him with songs, games, and dancing, they seat Odysseus at the table as a guest of honor and feast him royally. When they have finished eating and drinking, it is time for him to repay his hosts. It is his turn to tell stories. He welcomes the opportunity:

> There is no boon in life more sweet, I say,
> than when a summer joy holds all the realm,
> and banqueters sit listening to a harper
> in a great hall, by rows of tables heaped
> with bread and roast meat, while a steward goes
> to dip up wine and brim your cups again.
> Here is the flower of life, it seems to me!
>
> But now you wish to know my cause for sorrow—
> and thereby give me cause for more.
> What shall I

say first? What shall I keep until the end?
The gods have tried me in a thousand ways.
But first my name: let that be known to you,
And if I pull away from pitiless death,
friendship will bind us, though my land lies far.
I am Laërtês' son, Odysseus.
                              Men hold me
formidable for guile in peace and war.

                                                          IX.1–21

In the next four books (IX–XII), Odysseus recounts his adventures; with the Lotus Eaters, the Kyklops, Skylla and Charybdis, and all the rest. Readers typically remember these famous stories as the heart of the *Odyssey*. But a simple point must be noted: it is Odysseus himself telling them. And he is doing so in a situation in which it is entirely in his self-interest to tell them well. For he must win over the Phaiákians and convince them to give him a ship in which to return home. Even more so, he hopes they will give him gifts so that he does not return as a poor man. There is thus good reason to approach his stories, however engaging they may be, with suspicion. Does he exaggerate and embellish what "really" happened? Are his stories fabricated whole cloth as he tries to impress his audience? Whatever the answers, Odysseus' stories succeed magnificently. As the king says—and here Homer has him interrupt Odysseus' narrative, as if to remind his audience that they have been listening to a story—

                    As I so command—
        as sure as it I who, while I live,
        rule the sea rovers of Phaiákia. Our friend
        longs to put out for home, but let him be
        content here one more day, until
        I see all gifts bestowed. And every man
        will take thought for his launching and his voyage,
        I most of all, for I am master here.

                                                          XI.405–12

Strikingly, the king seems aware that Odysseus' stories may be too good to be true:

        From all we see, we take you for no swindler—
        though the dark earth be patient of so many,
        scattered everywhere, baiting their traps with lies
        of old times and of places no one knows.
        You speak with art, but your intent is honest.

The Argive troubles, and your own troubles,
You told as a poet would, a man who knows the world.

XI.421-7

Odysseus, says the king (to translate more literally), is able to give "shape to words": he speaks like poet or a singer who crafts his material well. Nonetheless, the king allows that "within you is a noble mind." Even though your stories are fantastic, he seems to be saying, I really like them. And you. In fact, "I could stay up until the sacred Dawn/ as long as you might wish to tell your story" (XI.437-8).

The point: the *Odyssey* is a story about a storyteller. It is a fiction about a man brilliant in crafting fictions. In no other work (that I know) is storytelling itself so decisively put on center stage. The *Odyssey* is also the "eatingest epic." Feasting with friends and strangers at the table is its recurrent leitmotif. In no other work (that I know) do food and wine, and the utensils for serving them, receive such loving attention. The connection between these two should now be clear. Both are fundamental responses to the Protean flux of our lives. We eat to maintain, however briefly, our form, and in enjoying our meals together we affirm the fact that we are all in the same (sinking) boat. Similarly, for at least as long as our memories hold up, we tell stories to give ourselves a sense of personal identity and unity. Both activities (briefly) save us from drowning in the fluid undercurrents of reality. And the *Odyssey*, the story of a hero who rejects immortality in favor of transience, celebrates both.

Odysseus and his crew, he tells the captivated audience of feasting Phaiákians, were on the sea, returning from Troy, and they suffered many a painful loss. The first was on the island of Ismaros, where they battled the Kikonês, who killed several of Odysseus' men. Strikingly, this bloodshed was caused by a bad mistake they made in their eating. After successfully plundering the island, Odysseus, fearing its inhabitants might attack, ordered his crew to return immediately to their ships. But,

My men were mutinous,
fools, on stores of wine. Sheep after sheep
they butchered by the surf, and shambling cattle,
feasting.

IX.51-4

Sure enough, just as ever mindful Odysseus feared, a large party of Kikonês returned and the bloodshed was terrible. As so often in the *Odyssey*, bad things happen to people who eat badly. Indeed, this is precisely what occurs in his next story as well: the Lotus Eaters. These gentle souls offer their visitors the "honeyed plant, the Lotos." Those who foolishly imbibed it "longed to stay forever, browsing on/ that native bloom, forgetful of their homeland" (IX.106–9). Like the opiate with which Helen spiked the wine, this one obliterates consciousness of past and future. Odysseus had to force these men, stoned out of their minds, to return to the ships.

The third story, far more elaborate than the first two, is of Polyphêmos, the Kyklops, and the son of Poseidon. Odysseus and his crew stumble upon his cave. Hungry after wandering on the sea for many days, they are delighted to find it uninhabited but filled with good stuff to eat: cheeses, lambs, and whey. The men urge Odysseus to snatch the plentiful food and return to the ship. But Odysseus, ever curious, orders them to remain. He wants not only to find out who lives in such a rugged place but also to learn whether he might be a generous host willing to give him gifts. Sure enough, the monster returns. After depositing the load of wood he was carrying, he then closes the entrance to the cave by placing a huge boulder in front of it. Odysseus, never one to be cowed, addresses him:

> We are from Troy, Akhaians, blown off course
> by shifting gales on the Great South Sea;
> homeward bound, but taking routes and ways
> uncommon; so the will of Zeus would have it.
> We served under Agamemnon, son of Atreus—
> The whole world knows what city
> he laid waste, what armies he destroyed.
> It was our luck to come here; here we stand,
> beholden for your help, or any gifts
> you give—as custom is to honor strangers.
> We would entreat you, great Sir, have a care
> for the gods' courtesy; Zeus will avenge
> the unoffending guest.
>
> IX.281–93

Odysseus is shocked by the monster's reply: he has no intention of abiding by the guest code. Not only does he refuse to feed his visitors, he eats two of them.

> Neither reply nor pity came from him,
> but in one stride he clutched at my companions
> and caught two in his hands like squirming puppies
> to beat their brains out, spattering the floor.
> Then he dismembered them and made his meal,
> gaping and crunching like a mountain lion—
> everything: innards, flesh, and marrow bones.
>
> IX.312–19

Polyphêmos is the worst of all villains because he is the worst of all eaters. A savage, he defies every conceivable norm of civilized life. Upon witnessing him eat his comrades, Odysseus' first impulse is to kill him on the spot, and so he draws his sword. But he quickly realizes that if he were to do so, then he and his men would be unable to move the enormous boulder the monster used to seal the entrance, and they would be trapped in the cave. In an act of astonishing self-control, he returns his sword to its scabbard. He then hatches a plot. First, he gets the Kyklops drunk. This is easy, since the uncivilized brute has no agriculture, and so no experience with the fruit of the vine. Then Odysseus tells him, "Nohbdy is my name" (IX.366). (In Greek, the word for "nobody," *outis*, sounds a bit like "Odysseus.") Finally, when the monster collapses in a stupor—"drunk, hiccuping,/ he dribbled streams of liquor and bits of men" (IX.405)—Odysseus takes a long spike, heats its tip to the burning point in the fire, and then stabs his one eye. The blinded Polyphêmos opens the boulder door of his cave, stumbles out, and then roars in pain: "Nohbdy, Nohbdy's tricked me. Nohbdy's ruined me!" (IX.445). Naturally, none of his fellow monsters pay him any mind. Odysseus, deeply pleased with himself— even though it was his own decision to stay in the cave that caused the death of several of his men—"was filled with laughter" (IX.451). Finally, the crew escapes by clinging to the bellies of Polyphêmos' sheep when they exit the cave.

It's a great story, regardless of whether it "really" happened. And it is one of the few instances where, in a weird sense, Odysseus speaks the truth. He really is a "nohbdy," precisely because he is the storyteller, the chameleon who changes his colors when needed, the master of flexible disguise, the sweet-talker, the liar. He is the fabricator of multiple identities to none of which he clings.

Another scene brings this feature of Nohbdy-Odysseus into sharp focus. With the generous help of the Phaiákians, he has finally made it back to Ithaka. But when he lands, having been gone for twenty years, he does not even recognize the place. Fortunately, Athena is there to help him. Disguised as a young shepherd, she tells him where he is. Odysseus is delighted—he "laughed in his heart, hearing his land described/ by Pallas Athena, daughter of Zeus" (XIII.320)—but intensely cautious. After all, he does not know who has been in charge in his homeland during his absence and what threats he will face. And so he concocts an elaborate tale. He tells Athena he is a man from Crete. Of course, the goddess sees right through his deception. But rather than be annoyed, she is pleased.

At this the grey-eyed goddess
Athena smiled, and gave him a caress,
her looks being changed now, so she seemed a woman,
tall and beautiful and no doubt skilled
at weaving splendid things. She answered briskly:

"Whoever gets around you must be sharp
and guileful as a snake; even a god
might bow to you in ways of dissimulation.
You! You chameleon!
Bottomless bag of tricks! Here in your own country
would you not give your stratagems a rest
Or stop spell binding for an instant?

You play a part as if it were your own tough skin.

No more of this, though. Two of a kind, we are,
contrivers, both. Of all men now alive
you are the best in plots and story telling.
My own fame is for wisdom among the gods—
deceptions, too."

XIII.365–84

It takes one to know one, and here we see two supremely talented liars delighting in each other's company.

There is another moment, this one troubling, when we see that Athena was exactly right about Odysseus: he cannot give his "stratagems a rest." After having successfully vanquished the suitors, he sets out to find his aged father, Laërtês, who has been living in self-imposed poverty and isolation for many years.

This was the figure Prince Odysseus found—
wasted by years, racked, bowed under grief.
The son paused by a tall pear tree and wept,
then inwardly debated: should he run
forward and kiss his father, and pour out
his tale of war, adventure and return,
or should he first interrogate him, test him?

Better that way, he thought—
first draw him out with sharp words, trouble him.

XXIV.257–66

Up to this moment, Odysseus had good reason to be extremely cautious in Ithaka. His palace had been under siege, and he no longer knew whom he could trust. He was thus continually on guard, and in disguise, as he executed his plot to vanquish the suitors. But now the battle is over, and he has won. Nonetheless, he still lies to his own father. He tells an elaborate story in which he identifies himself as "Quarrelman" (XXIV.337), a sailor whose ship inadvertently landed in Ithaka. It simply is not clear why he does so, for surely Laërtês is no threat. Perhaps Odysseus just cannot stop lying. Perhaps he is addicted to his own storytelling.

The danger of story addiction is captured perfectly in Odysseus' tale of the Sirens, whose singing can blow a man's "mind away" and cause him to forget to eat or drink.

> There are bones
> of dead men rotting in a pile beside them
> and flayed skins shrivel around the spot.
>
> XII.52–5

Having been forewarned about these gorgeously diabolical singers, Odysseus has his crew tie him to the mast of his ship, and plug up their own ears with beeswax to prevent them from succumbing. Only he himself is allowed to listen. (And of what do the Sirens sing? "Of Troy" (XII.234), of course.) Stories give us a stable sense of identity and are thus of vital importance, but they have the potential to spin out of control and take over our lives. (The same goes for food and, especially, wine.)

VI Identity and Names

"No man is nameless" (VIII.590)—so says Alkinoös when he reminds Odysseus of the rules of the guest code. Only after the host bathes, clothes, and feeds the stranger, and makes sure he has something to drink, is he permitted to ask for his name. And the stranger is then required not only to give it to him but also to tell a little life story in order to flesh it out. Were he not to do so, he would be a nobody.

Nowhere is naming more fully, even if tragically, put into play than in Odysseus' showdown with Polyphêmos. After having successfully tricked the monster, and gotten his men out of the cave and to their ship, Odysseus finally sets to sea. But before his crew row too far from shore, he cannot resist boasting of his victory:

O Kyklops! Would you feast on my companions?
Puny, am I, in a Caveman's hands?
How do you like the beating that we gave you,
you damned cannibal? Eater of guests
under your roof! Zeus and the gods have paid you!

IX.519–24

Even though he is now blind, the giant responds by throwing boulders in the direction of the voice, and they land close to the ship. The men just want to get away. But Odysseus insists on talking more trash to Polyphêmos. His men beg him not to: "Godsake, Captain!/ Why bait the beast again? Let him alone!" (IX.539). Odysseus ignores them:

> Kyklops,
> if ever mortal man inquire
> how you were put to shame and blinded, tell him
> Odysseus, raider of cities, took your eye:
> Laërtês' son, whose home's on Ithaka.

IX.549–54

Polyphêmos, now knowing the name of his enemy, prays to his father, the god Poseidon, that Odysseus never be allowed to return home. And if this request cannot be met, at least "let him lose all companions, and return/ under strange sail to bitter days at home" (IX.586–7). Poseidon grants the latter, and hurls so many storms at Odysseus' ship that it is repeatedly blown off course, and the crew is faced with ever more deadly struggles. At the end, only Odysseus—who, if his own story is to be believed, seems to be an abject failure as a leader of men—makes it to Skerhía, and then back home to Greece, alive.

Who is Odysseus? The son of Laërtês who grew up in Ithaka and became the raider of cities? Or is he Nohbdy? Both. For, as this scene strikingly illustrates, the former is extracted from the latter. Odysseus, enraged at Polyphêmos, desperate not only to exact revenge but also to be recognized as having done so, insists upon identifying himself in order to receive credit for his triumph. On the one hand, this is a terrible mistake. On the other, he has no choice. Because we are irrevocably implicated in the passage of time and are fading away even as we speak, we need stories to give us a semblance of stability and wholeness. And we need names to which we attach these stories and with which we identify ourselves. Finally, we need an audience to hear our stories. While we can, indeed we must, function as audiences to ourselves in order to maintain a sense of personal identity, it is also necessary to be heard, to be recognized, by another.

VII Recognitions

There are splendid recognition scenes in Homer's *Odyssey*. So, for example, when Telémakhos finally returns to Ithaka from his journey to the home of Meneláos, he first visits Eumaios, the loyal swineherd, who at that very moment is hosting Odysseus, who has just returned from Skhería. Ever cautious, Odysseus is in disguise and initially does not reveal himself to his son. Finally, though, Athena orders him to "dissemble to your son no longer" (XVI.195), and so, dispensing with pretense, he declares to Telémakhos,

> I am that father whom your boyhood lacked
> and suffered pain for lack of. I am he.
>
> > XVI.221–2

The boy, never having even seen his father, is incredulous, and, much like his father, does not drop his guard. So Odysseus reiterates his claim:

> This is not princely, to be swept
> away by wonder at your father's presence.
> No other Odysseus will ever come,
> for he and I are one, the same; his bitter
> fortune and his wanderings are mine.
> Twenty years gone, and I am back again
> On my own island.
>
> > XVI.239–45

Odysseus is one and the same, even though twenty years have passed, and Telémakhos sees him as such. His father is his father, regardless of how much time has passed.

Another: When Odysseus returns to his palace, disguised as a beggar, and begins to put his plan to annihilate the suitors into motion, he is recognized by his old dog, Argos, who "pricked up his ears/ and lifted up his muzzle" (XVII.374) at the sight of his beloved master. And then, perhaps to avoid inadvertently revealing Odysseus' identity, he died.

Or this: Odysseus' childhood nurse, Eurykleia, having been ordered to bathe him, disguised as a miserable beggar, sees the scar on his thigh, which she remembers from decades ago. "She knew the groove at once" (XIX.455) and proclaims,

> *You are Odysseus!* Ah, dear child! I could not
> see you until now—not till I knew
> my master's very body with my hands!
>
> > XIX.549–51

The most elaborate recognition scene of all occurs between Odysseus and his wife. His relentless drive to make sail for home is ultimately successful, and awaiting him is faithful Penelope, keeper of the flame. She loves her husband, and so has resolutely rebuffed the suitors for many years. Perhaps, then, she represents what is truly stable in human life: an abiding home in which we are surrounded by those who know us for who we really are.

Yes, the *Odyssey* is a story of homecoming, and Penelope's recognition of her husband does indeed take place. But the situation is more complicated than it might seem. As Homer makes clear, soon after returning to Ithaka, Odysseus will once again have to leave. This was foretold by the prophet Teirêsias. Odysseus met him when he visited Hades, the land of the dead. (Or so he said when he was telling tales to the Phaiákians.)

> But after you have dealt out death—in open
> combat or by stealth—to all the suitors,
> go overland on foot, and take an oar,
> until one day you come where men have lived
> with meat unsalted, never known the sea,
> nor seen seagoing ships, with crimson bows
> and oars that fledge light hulls for dipping flight.
> The spot will soon be plain to you, and I
> Can tell you how: some passerby will say,
> "What winnowing fan is that upon your shoulder?"
> Halt, and implant your smooth oar in the turf
> and make fair sacrifice to Lord Poseidon.
>
> XI.133–46

To make amends to Poseidon, Teirêsias tells him, Odysseus must travel to a place whose inhabitants are so unfamiliar with ships that they think an oar is a winnowing fan. Now, Ithaka is a rather small island. Surely all of its inhabitants know something about the sea and seafaring. As soon as he returns home, then, Odysseus must leave on a voyage to find a landlocked place greatly distant from any shore. No easy trip.

Still, it is arguable that Penelope and the marriage bed represent what abides in an otherwise unruly life. After all, Teirêsias also predicts that Odysseus will die at home "wearied out with rich old age" (XI.150). Homer seems to suggest as much when he has Odysseus describe the bed itself.

> No mortal
> in his best days could budge it with a crowbar.
> There is our pact and pledge, our secret sign,

built into that bed—my handiwork
and no one else's!
        An old trunk of olive
grew like a pillar on the building plot,
and I laid out our bedroom round that tree,
lined up the stone walls, built the walls and roof,
gave it a doorway and smooth-fitting doors.

XXIII.211–20

Like an immovable pillar, the olive tree trunk is the foundation of the bed. The walls of the room surrounding it are stone. The image is of solidity and reliability. Surely, then, these features belong to family and home. And yet the story, as revealed by the long scene in which Penelope finally recognizes Odysseus, is not simple.

The first move comes when Odysseus, still in disguise—this time as Aithon from Crete—tells Penelope that he had once entertained Odysseus at his home. As usual, his ruse is successful.

Now all these lies he made appear so truthful
she wept as she sat listening. The skin
of her pale face grew moist the way pure snow
softens and glistens on the mountains, thawed
by Southwind after powdering from the West,
and, as the snow melts, mountain streams run full:
so her white cheeks were wetted by these tears
shed for her lord—and he close by her side.

XIX.240–9

Penelope had been ice, frozen in a defensive stance to protect herself against the aggression of the suitors and the enormous insecurity she has suffered for so many years. But hearing an apparently first-hand report about her husband begins to soften her. Nevertheless, Odysseus/Aithon, despite the swell of feeling he experiences, refuses to reveal himself.

Imagine how his heart ached for his lady,
his wife in tears; and yet he never blinked;
his eyes might have been made of horn or iron
for all that she could see. He has this trick—
wept, if he willed to, inwardly.

XIX.240–50

After the initial melt, Penelope herself also hardens, and she immediately asks her visitor to give her some proof he has actually met Odysseus. What, she asks him, was he wearing? Of course, Odysseus/Aithon gives the right answer, and in detail: a purple cloak, a golden brooch, a lovely shirt. Upon hearing all this, Penelope weeps again. Odysseus/Aithon tries to cheer her with a lengthy story and a promise that not only is her husband alive and well, but he is heading homeward as they speak. Still, hardened by her years alone, she remains (like her husband) supremely cautious and guarded.

> Ah, stranger,
> if what you say could ever happen!
> You would soon know our love! Our bounty, too:
> Men would turn after you to call you blessed.
> But my hearts tells me what must be.
> Odysseus will not come to me; no ship
> will be prepared for you. We have no master
> quick to receive and furnish out a guest
> as Lord Odysseus was.
> Or did I dream him?
>
> XIX.366–75

Memories, especially those shared by no one else, are easy to doubt. Are they real or might they be dreams? Such is Penelope's confusion. She has been having vivid dreams lately, and she asks the stranger to interpret one of them. An eagle, claiming to be her husband, swoops down and kills her twenty geese. What could be more self-explanatory? The geese are the suitors. But Penelope refuses to grant the dream its obvious meaning. "Friend," she says, "many and many a dream is mere confusion,/ a cobweb of no consequence at all" (XIX.650). Despite the reassurances of Odysseus/Aithon, she is on the edge of despair. She has, after all, been alone for twenty years, and so she announces that, at last, she is willing to marry someone else. She proposes a contest:

> I shall decree a contest for the day.
> We have twelve axe heads. In his time, my lord
> could line them up, all twelve, at intervals
> like a ship's ribbing; then he'd back away
> a long away off and whip an arrow through.
> Now I'll impose this trial on the suitors.
> The one who easily handles and strings the bow
> and shoots through all twelve axes I shall marry.
>
> XIX.664–75

Penelope here imagines a time when she finally says goodbye to the life she had with her husband. "But I'll remember, though I dream it only" (XIX.676). In fact, the very next night she dreams of Odysseus just before he left for Troy:

> Tonight the image of my lord came by
> as I remember him with troops. O strange
> exultation! I thought him real, not a dream.

XX.98–100

At this very moment, however, Odysseus has actually returned and has commenced his assault on the suitors. Strangely, Penelope was sleeping peacefully while the furious battle was taking place in her own courtyard. When she is awakened by her maid and told the joyous news that Odysseus not only has returned but has killed all their enemies, she refuses to believe her.

> Penelope said:
> "Dear nurse … the gods have touched you.
> They can put chaos into the clearest head
>
> or bring a lunatic down to earth. Good sense
> you always had. They've touched you. What is this
> mockery you wake up to tell me,
> breaking in on my sweet spell of sleep?
> I had not dozed away so tranquilly
> since my lord went to war.

XXIII.14–21

This entire scene is infused with a murky blend of memory and dream. Penelope simply does not know what is really happening, what she thinks or remembers. (Or so she says.) Even when she finally sees her husband, covered in blood, even when she hears the nurse's description of his telltale scar, she still refuses to succumb to the temptation of belief. "If he is truly Odysseus, and he has come home, then we shall find other ways, and better, to recognize each other" (XXIII.107–10). She will test her husband, a prospect that delights Odysseus, for in her caution and guard he sees a reflection of himself. Admiringly, he says to her,

> Strange woman,
> the immortals of Olympos made you hard,
> harder than any. Who else in the world
> would keep aloof as you do from her husband
> if he returned to her from years of trouble,
> cast on his own land in the twentieth year?

XXIII.186–92

Penelope then tricks the trickster. She tells the nurse to put their bed "outside the bedchamber" (XXIII.204). Of course, this is impossible. The bed is anchored in the tree trunk, a secret known only to husband and wife. The ruse works, for Odysseus snaps and declares that "no mortal/ in his best days could" move the sturdy bed. Since only he would know this, he has passed the test. The recognition is complete, and Penelope's

> knees
> grew tremulous and weak, her heart failed her.
> With eyes brimming with tears she ran to him,
> throwing her arms around his neck, and kissed him,
> murmuring:
> > "Do not rage at me,
> > > Odysseus!"
> > > > XXIII.232–23

This is the first time in the *Odyssey* she calls him by his name, and when she does, he, finally, breaks into tears. They embrace, and then Athena, god bless her, "slowed the night/ when night was most profound, and held the Dawn/ under the Ocean of the East" (XXIII.274–6). Athena stops time. Does this mean that love stops time? Unfortunately not. After their lovemaking, Odysseus tells his wife, "One trial—I do not know how long—is left for me to see fulfilled. Teirêsias's ghost forewarned me" (XXIII.280). After having been gone for twenty years, and after having been but one night at home, he has already announced his impending departure. And after he has gone, will he return or will he, yet again, become no more than a dream to her?

The point: yes, we are somebodies who can be recognized and loved by those closest to us, and who call us by our names. Such recognitions nourish us throughout our lives, and without them we would dwindle. But they will not last, for they depend on the human capacity to forge an identity. Odysseus' willful, and apparently stupid, declaration of his name to Polyphêmos is emblematic. We must announce ourselves to, thrust ourselves into, the world by dint of our own energy. We must keep ourselves intact by imposing form on what otherwise would be no more than Protean flux. Our identities, like all forms and well-crafted stories, are fictions we generate to keep ourselves afloat. Yes, they are real. Hearing the words, "Tell him Odysseus, raider of cities, took your eye," Polyphêmos knows who blinded him, and so can exact vengeance upon him. Odysseus' identity is thus as real as the suffering he endures at the hands of Poseidon. Of course, those sufferings are only as real as the stories Odysseus, drawing either from his storehouse of memories or his imagination, tells.

VIII The Shades in Hades

Hades, the land of the dead, provokes another challenge to the reading of the *Odyssey* being developed here. For in Book XI the dead surely seem to live on. After all, Odysseus (telling his tales to the dinner party of rapt Phaiákians) claims that he spoke with them when he visited the place. Perhaps, then, transience, the passing away of all we are and have, is not the Homeric bottom line. Again, however, things are not always what they seem.

The words Homer uses to describe the shadowy beings who inhabit Hades are almost all negative. They are "blurred and breathless" (XI.30) and "bereft of all the reach and power" (460) they had when alive. They are "cold" (105), and so need the living to warm them up. They cannot speak unless they drink the blood of the animals Odysseus sacrificed. ("Any dead man/ whom you allow to enter where the blood is/ will speak to you" (166).) They are "exhausted" (581), "dimwitted" (560), and no more than "the after images of used-up men" (561).

Homer, at least in Fitzgerald's translation, calls the dead "souls" (40). This English word, however, is potentially misleading. For it suggests a substantial entity capable of existing without the body. By contrast, the Greek word is *psuchê*, whose origin is *psuchein*, "to breathe" (and which is the ancestor of our words "psyche" and "psychology"). For Homer, then, the *psuchê* is the breath of life, the animating principle of a living being. When a man breathes his last, his *psuchê* leaves him. And then his corpse is motionless and gradually begins to decompose and merge with its surrounding environment. *Psuchê* in the *Odyssey* is the life force that keeps an animal intact, and so is not well translated by "soul."

Consider, for example, the moment in Hades when Odysseus sees the "soul" of his mother, who died of heartbreak because her son did not return home. He tries to hug her. "But she went sifting through my hands, impalpable/ as shadows are" (XI.232). Unlike the "souls" that, say, Dante describes in the *Inferno*— full-throated characters who retain their identities as they endure eternal punishment—his mother is no more than shadow. And the salient feature of a shadow is precisely its lack of independent reality: it depends on another object to cast it. If the object (or the light source) is removed, then it disappears.

Another simile: Homer's dead "waver like a dream" (XI.232). Or, as Odysseus' mother puts it, "dreamlike the soul flies, insubstantial" (XI.253). And a dream, of course, depends on the dreamer. Just as Penelope's dreams flitted between clarity and murk, reality and fantasy, despair and hope, so too do the Homeric dead. At times they may seem really real. But they are not.

There is another superbly expressive word Homer uses to describe the dead. Odysseus sees Elpenor, a comrade who, having gotten drunk and then fallen off a ladder, died but was never buried. When he appears, he is just a "faint image" (XI.93). Like dream and shadow, an image (in Greek, an *eidolon*) depends on something else—call it the "original"—for its existence. Think of a picture of a friend you see on your phone. It looks like her, but you know it is only a picture. For one thing, what you see on the screen is two-dimensional and your friend is three-dimensional. Still, seeing the image you also see, in your mind's eye, or your memory, your friend. Seeing an image on the phone, then, is really a kind of double-seeing. For you see not only an illuminated shape, but you see it as an image of something else: the real thing—your living, breathing friend. The image, which is of something other than itself, reminds you of the original, compared to which it falls short.

Even if an image is utterly second-rate in its reality, it nonetheless can look a lot like its original. As such, it can confuse us. Now, it's doubtful that you will ever try to hug the picture of your friend appearing on the screen. But other images are more convincing. Think, for example, of our relationship to celebrities. We never actually meet them in the flesh, but nonetheless we often fool ourselves into thinking that, because we track their lives in the media, we actually know something about this movie star or that famous athlete. In fact, however, all we have access to is their appearances on our screens. It hardly needs to be said that the same holds true of our political leaders.

In sum, Homer's depiction of the "souls" in Hades—shadows, dreams, images—offers no real solace for those who might despair at the prospect of their inevitable demise. No one expresses this thought better than Achilles, the greatest warrior of the Greeks. Odysseus greets him warmly:

> But was there ever a man more blest by fortune
> than you, Akhilleus? Can there ever be?
> We ranked you with immortals in your lifetime,
> we Argives did, and here your power is royal
> among the dead men's shades. Think, then, Akhilleus:
> You need not be so pained by death.
>
> XI.569–75[4]

Through his magnificent exploits on the battlefield, Achilles had achieved the highest possible goal of a Homeric hero: he had won fame and glory, and so his name will live on in the memories of others. But as he tells Odysseus, this now matters to him not at all:

Let me hear no smooth talk
of death from Odysseus, light of councils.
Better, I say, to bread sod as a farm hand
for some poor country man, on iron rations,
than lord it over all the exhausted dead.

XI.577–81

These are shocking words coming from a Greek warrior-aristocrat, for they fly in the face of a heroic culture in which great men demand acknowledgment of their superiority. Now in Hades, Achilles would like nothing more than simply to be alive, even if he were no more than a servant of a pathetically poor farmer. There is nothing positive in being dead, and he refuses to allow Odysseus, storyteller (form-maintainer) par excellence, to convince him otherwise, to bamboozle him yet again.

Achilles understands that his life as a warrior-hero pursuing honor and glory was, in effect, a quest for metaphorical immortality. When he was alive, he wanted to live on in the memories and stories of future generations. But now dead, he recognizes such a quest for what it really was: meaningless.[5] Yes, we sing his praises even today! But this does not make him alive, for he now exists only in our memories, and these too will fade. Like a dream, a shadow, or an image, the ghost of Achilles has but a parasitical existence.

The shades in Hades need the blood of an animal to speak. Translated into realistic terms, the dead need the living to remember and tell stories about them in order to be brought back to life. For only such is available to them, and it is barely a whisper. This, finally, is Homer's version of Hades. It is not like Dante's *Inferno*, a place of souls. It is a symbolic representation of memory and imagination. When we die we disappear. If we are lucky, someone in the future might recall what we did well, or might tell a story about us, and perhaps embellish it beautifully. Or dream of us. Next to nothing, but not nothing.

IX Justice in the *Odyssey*

In its own way, the *Odyssey* is an intensely moral book. A set of principles, firm and abiding, seems to govern it from start to finish. Odysseus formulates one: "No man should flout the law,/ but keep in peace what gifts the gods may give" (XVIII.175). Failure to heed this imperative brings severe retribution. "The gods/ living in bliss are fond of no wrongdoing,/ but honor discipline and right behavior" (XIV.100–3). In other words, bad guys get what's coming to them, while good guys seem to win out in the end. Or as Odysseus puts it, "fair dealing brings more profit in the end" (XXII.420). Only in a world governed by justice would this be true. Is justice, then, an island of stability in an ocean of flux? If so, it would challenge the reading of the *Odyssey* offered here so far.

Strikingly, but no longer surprisingly, food plays a critical role in determining what counts as "law," "fair dealing," or "right behavior." For the most basic moral requirement is to treat strangers and beggars well, and this means, first and foremost, to feed them. On the one hand, the reason why is straightforward. Nausikaa, lovely princess of the Phaiákians, explains, "Strangers and beggars/ come from Zeus." They are under the protection of the greatest of all gods and, as such, implicitly merit good treatment. There is also a prudential side to this moral imperative:

> You know they go in foreign guise, the gods do,
> looking like strangers, turning up
> in towns and settlements to keep an eye
> on manners, good and bad.
>
> XVII.634–7

A stranger or beggar must be treated well because, who knows, he might be Athena. No one's identity is completely stable. We are all nobodies who construct a fiction, wear a mask, in order to maintain a sense of ourselves. In other words, we are all strangers. Meneláos articulated this point (in a passage cited earlier) when he rebuked Eteóneus for failing to invite Telémakhos and Peisístratos to join them for dinner.

> Could we have made it home again—and Zeus
> give us no more hard roving!—if other men
> had never fed us, given us lodging?
>
> IV.33–9

We're all in the same (sinking) boat, and so we must recognize our shared humanity and take care of one another. We must treat strangers as if they were family. Such is the singular imperative of Homeric morality.

Melánthios, the goatherd who is at the beck and call of the suitors, is someone who utterly fails to abide by this standard. When he encounters a beggar, not recognizing that he is actually Odysseus in disguise, he mocks him as being a lazy bum who just doesn't want to work.

He'd rather tramp the country
begging, to keep his hoggish belly full.
Well, I can tell you this for sure:
in King Odysseus' hall, if he goes there,
footstools will fly around his head—good shots
from strong hands. Back and side, his ribs will catch it
on the way out.

XVII.291–8

Sure enough, when Odysseus, still disguised as a beggar, finally enters his own palace, the suitor Antínoös throws a footstool at him.

When an actual beggar, "a true scavenger … a public tramp" (XVIII.1), a man named Iros, comes to the palace, Antínoös forces him to enter a boxing match with (the still disguised) Odysseus. With utter cruelty he pits two (apparently) pitiful men against each other for his own amusement. Odysseus, of course, could smash Iros to smithereens if he wished, but he only gives him "a gentle blow" (XVIII.114), both to spare the poor lout and to conceal his real strength. Still, the blow he delivers breaks Iros' jaw. And when they saw this, the suitors "whooped and swung their arms, half dead/ with pangs of laughter" (XVIII.122). Their behavior is repugnant, and they will pay dearly for breaking the rules. As Odysseus tried to explain to the savage Polyphêmos, "Zeus will avenge/ the unoffending guest" (IX.281–93). And so Antínoös will be killed in an exquisitely appropriate manner. He will be shot with an arrow just as he is about to drink some wine.

Melánthios too will get what he deserves. After being killed, his corpse will be mutilated. His nose, ears, hands, feet, and genitals will be cut off "to feed the dogs" (XXII.528).

The point here is not to extol the *Odyssey* as a masterpiece of morality. For it is terribly brutal. So, for example, even Leódes, a suitor who had felt "shame" at the behavior of his companions and "could not abide their manners" (XXI.165), must be killed. He begs Odysseus for mercy: "Never by word or act of mine, I swear,/ was any woman troubled here. I told the rest/ to put an end to it. They would not listen" (XXII.351–3). To no avail does he plead. For as Odysseus tells him, just before he cuts his throat, "You were the diviner to this crowd … Death it shall be" (XXII.365). Or consider the fate of the young maids in the palace. Their offense was to party with the suitors.

They would be hung like doves
or larks in springès triggered in a thicket,
where the birds think to rest—a cruel nesting.

So now in turn each woman thrust her head
into a noose and swung, yanked high in air,
to perish there most piteously.
Their feet danced for a little, but not for long.

XXII.519–25

The image, the last line in particular, is hard to stomach. These were but poor, foolish girls only having some fun. So, no, the point here is not to praise the *Odyssey* for its commitment to justice. Instead, it is only to suggest that it has one. Bad guys meet a cruel but, in the eyes of the poet at least, a just fate.

Does justice itself, then, however brutally cold it may sometimes be, provide the stability otherwise missing in human life? Might the moral law of retribution be a permanent feature of the world we inhabit? Maybe. But if so it is not some rock-hard ideal separated from the vicissitudes of human life. Instead, it is manifested in the actions of human beings trying to stay afloat. For its primordial manifestation is bound to the most elemental embodiment of our transience: food. The paradigmatically moral act is to eat well, and this requires inviting others—friends, families, beggars, and especially strangers—to join at the table.

Eumaios, the most loyal servant in Odysseus' household, illustrates this theme especially well. He had been banished by the suitors, who forced him to tend the pigs and supply them with pork. But when Odysseus returns, having just arrived in Ithaka and disguised as a beggar, and he stumbles upon the meager hut Eumaios has built for himself in the woods, the old man comes to life. He invites the stranger in:

Come to the cabin. You're a wanderer too.
You must eat something, drink some wine, and tell me
Where you are from and the hard times you've seen.

XIV.52–4

These words mark Eumaios as a good man who understands the Homeric code in his bones. He even recites the same formula articulated by Nausikaa: "All wanderers/ and beggars come from Zeus." Eumaios does not have much to offer, but this does not deter him from sharing.

He tucked his long shirt up inside his belt
and strode into the pens for two young porkers.
He slaughtered them and singed them at the fire,
flayed and quartered them, and skewered the meat
to broil it all; then gave it to Odysseus

hot on the spits. He shook out barley meal,
took a winebowl of ivy wood and filled it,
and sat down facing him, with a gesture, saying;

"There is your dinner, friend, the pork of slaves.
Our fat shoats are all eaten by the suitors,
cold-hearted men, who never spare a thought
for how they stand in the sight of Zeus."

                                                    XIV.90–102

Before eating, Eumaios says this:

Bless you, stranger, fall to and enjoy it
for what it is. Zeus grants us this or that,
or else refrains from granting, as he wills;
all things are in his power.

                                                    XIV.522–5

Life is ineliminably precarious. What is here today is sure to be gone tomorrow. So enjoy your supper. Beautiful words from a beautiful man. No wonder he, along with Odysseus and Telémakhos, are victorious at the end. No wonder the suitors will be slaughtered while Eumaios will be restored to his rightful place in the palace. He is a good guy.

There is, however, another side to Homeric justice. It requires revenge. However brutal the killings of Leódes and the young maids may be, they are not frowned upon. For the victims had been disloyal to the household, and in some sense they deserved their fate. There is, however, an inevitable dark side to revenge. It generates a response in kind. This is precisely what occurs at the end of the *Odyssey*. Having killed so many of Ithaka's young aristocrats, Odysseus must face the wrath of their fathers and brothers. Eupeithês, father of Antínoös, leads the charge and exhorts his fellows to attack Odysseus:

Up with you! After him!—
before he can take flight to Pylos town
or hide at Elis, under Epeian law!
We'd be disgraced forever! Mocked for generations
if we cannot avenge our sons' blood, and our brothers'!
Life would turn to ashes—at least for me;
rather be dead and join the dead.

                                                    XXIV.472–9

On a different occasion, Odysseus himself might have uttered these very words. After all, he himself was animated by precisely this sentiment when he joined forces with his son and the loyal swineherd to attack the suitors. The cycle of revenge relentlessly repeats. As if to signal the utter futility, and terrible costs, of such a system, Homer ends the *Odyssey* abruptly. Just after old Laertes, newly invigorated and thrilled at the prospect of killing his enemies, slaughters Eupeithês with a mighty throw of his spear, Athena appears on the battlefield and proclaims, "Now hold!/ Break off this bitter skirmish;/ end your bloodshed Ithakans, and make peace" (XXIV.591–4). Instantly, the fighting stops and both parties agree to a peace treaty. Thus concludes the *Odyssey*.

A reader cannot help but wonder whether the story would better have ended in Book XXIII, when Odysseus and Penelope finally reunite and Athena halts the progress of the sun in order to give them more time in bed. Instead, it ends in an abrupt flash with a god intruding in human affairs to bring closure. (Call Athena's appearance a deus ex machina.) Perhaps, however, this strange ending fits the *Odyssey* perfectly, for it suggests that human affairs never actually reach tidy closure, achieve symmetry, or become solidly fastened with the bonds of justice. Yes, civil war has been averted in Ithaka. But the finale is not convincing. For surely there will be no lasting peace, no rest.

X The *Odyssey* as an Affirmation of Life

Homer's *Odyssey*, from its first word ("man") to its final scene, is a sustained attempt not only honestly to face, but also to affirm, the fragility of human existence, and to do so on its own terms, without recourse to hope in some beyond or for salvation. Just life.

Living beings are continually at work keeping themselves alive. To achieve this, they must interact with the environment immediately surrounding them. First, at least in the case of animals like us, they must breathe. Air is taken in, oxygen extracted, carbon dioxide released. Second, they must eat. Nutrients are ingested, digested, and waste products excreted. In this, the most basic life activity, what is other than the organism becomes the organism. The apple sitting on my table is different from me. After I have eaten it, it has disappeared as an independent entity. After I have digested it, it will supply energy to, and also actually become, me. Such is metabolism (from the Greek *metabolê*, which means "change"): the outside/other becoming the inside/same.

As long as an animal is alive, metabolic activity is continuous, and its material components are changing. Its cells are in perpetual flux as, say, this bit of oxygen comes in and that bit of carbon dioxide goes out. Despite this continual exchange, but also because of it, an animal persists as itself over time. It retains its boundaries and internal organization—its form. It remains intact and therefore distinct from its immediate environment. When metabolic activity ceases, the organism dies. What had been a living, breathing squirrel becomes, after it has been run over by a car, a chunk of matter soon to disintegrate. Alive, an animal continuously works precisely in order to prevent this, to maintain its physical integrity even as its body continually changes. This takes energy. When it runs out, as it inevitably will, the animal dies.

To valorize eating and elevate it to the central position in human affairs, as Homer so clearly does, is to affirm our animality, and to refuse to seek meaning or solace in anything beyond the life cycle itself. It is to affirm, even to celebrate, our transience.

Equally primordial is the human capacity for storytelling. Generating a narrative, forging an arrangement of incidents with a beginning, a middle, and an end, provides an identity that our lives, ever flowing, both require and eventually undermine. Unless we have a name to which we can append a little life story, unless we can fashion a coherent narrative from the resources supplied by our memory and direct it toward an imagined future, we will cease to be ourselves. The old man with severe dementia can no longer do this. Even though he is still breathing and eating, he is, in the deepest sense, nobody. Alive, at least for a while, we have the wherewithal to make something of ourselves. This takes work; this takes stories.

Finally, then, it is wise to heed the all too beautiful Helen when she urges us to combine these two fundamental versions of self-maintenance: "So take refreshment, take your ease in hall,/ and cheer the time with stories" (IV.255–6). The dinner party, with its good food, copious wine, and rollicking tales, tells us who we are: fragile beings who are in the same (sinking) boat. While it too will come to an end, and the dishes will have to be washed, it is the best we can do. Next to nothing, perhaps, but not nothing, and at least we are in it together. Such, at least, is the lesson of the "eatingest epic": Homer's *Odyssey*.

Interlude[1]

(2)

Yesterday, I burned the tomatoes. I had started the sauce when I got home around five. Before the garlic began to brown, I had added the tomatoes, from a can since it's still only spring. I sprinkled salt and lots of basil (dried, because ours has not yet started to grow). Kept a high heat, threw in a medium pat of butter, added white wine frequently, boiled it down to a thick, oily almost-paste. I turned the fire off and let it sit. My plan was to reignite the fire and add the shrimp to the pan after I put the pasta into boiling water.

It was unusually warm, and so I went to the front porch. This is where Gina and I spend almost every evening when the weather is fine. We have drinks, watch whatever semblance of the world goes by. Plenty of cars, but also some people. Usually with dogs, often with strollers. Almost always on the phone or connected by earbud to their private playlists. And then there are the runners. Neatly decked out in high-tech, tight-fitting gear, they glide by with varying degrees of proficiency. Even though we are quite visible on our porch, and usually have some music on while we sit, almost none of the passersby says hi or even looks our way.

Yesterday, though, I was alone. Warm sun and sipping a tall glass of cheap white wine on ice, wearing dark shades, tunes in the background, it was a rare moment for me. I relaxed a bit, sank into the chair, put my feet up, and just watched. The terrible urge to move was almost gone. My stream of consciousness, usually jumpy and dominated by reminders of what I have to do next, flowed more smoothly. I told myself stories, concocted elaborate fantasies, all the while just staring. The sun was going down behind the tall trees on the other side of the street, and leaf-shadows flickered on the porch. This reminded me of the Japanese woodcuts I've seen at the Museum of Fine Arts. And in the beam of sunlight that falls just to the side of the telephone pole, gnats glinted as they danced madly.

Gina came home on her bike. She lugged it up the stairs to the porch, and we smiled at each other. After locking it in the corner, she sat with me for a minute. She just got back from the gym and was hot and tired and did not want to move. But she had to get herself some wine, which meant she had to go into the house. While she was gone, I continued staring. When she returned, we each briefly recounted the inconsequential doings of our day. Then we fell silent and stared at the street. My glass soon was empty (again), and so I pushed myself up from the chair and went into the house for a refill. I figured that my tomatoes could use just a bit more heat, and so I turned the fire back on while I poked around in the refrigerator. My thought was to turn the burner off before I returned to the porch. But I forgot to do that. No surprise, I suppose. I was a bit smashed.

I came back to the porch and resumed my position. We talked a little as we drank. Then Gina asked, "Is something burning?" "Oh shit," I said when I realized what was going on. Sure enough, the pan was smoking and filled with blackened crud. Still, I was not upset. Truth be told, I can't remember when I last burned a dinner. If nothing else, my timing tends to the impeccable.

I cut the fire and took the pan off the stove. It wasn't hard to figure something else out to eat. Pasta with sharp pecorino Romano, pepper, and oil. Shrimp on the side, even though rumor has it that Italians do not mix seafood with cheese. And there were some peas, which have just come into season, and also a fine salad, all the greens coming from local greenhouses. Mesclun mix, arugula, and mustard, doused in oil and balsamic vinegar. Bitter, just the way I like it.

(3)

I've already been to the ATM to get a wad of cash, and in a few minutes I will ride my bike from my office to the Copley Square farmers' market. This will be nice. It's only late May but very warm. Since school is not in session, I'm wearing shorts and sandals. I'll ride on the esplanade along the Charles River, comfortably separated from cars. And now I'm imagining what to buy, and from whom I'll buy it. At Stillman's I'll get a bunch of sausages. Most I'll freeze, but some we'll cook for the dinner we're hosting on Sunday. They also have good potatoes. Quite dirty and in need of a lot of work—where have they been all winter?—but they have good flavor when roasted. Greens will come from Atlas Farms. Their mesclun mix is terrific, and I'll supplement it with some mustard to give it even more bite. The fields are not yet producing much on their own, but the farmers now use hoop houses, white cylindrical canopies, to cover small green plants and give them a head start on the growing season. I'll need to buy a lot since we also have two friends coming over tonight. Gina will be picking up some lamb chops, but I'm not sure from where. I'll get cheese from the German guy whose dairy is in New Hampshire. His blue is good, although not quite strong enough for my taste. Still, I enjoy chatting with him so I keep going back. The chips-and-salsa lady might be there this week. Her in-laws are from Mexico, and she runs a small factory in Somerville. If they're still available, best of all might be the asparagus from Siena Farms. Last week they were purplish and thick, and all I had to do was marinate and salt them before throwing them on the grill for a few minutes. Almost charred, they were delicious. It's such a short season for those guys, and I don't want to miss any of it. I'll be home by 2:30 and will then spend a couple of hours in the kitchen. I'll uncork the wine, an Amarone, and make sure there's a cold bottle of prosecco ready to go. Our friends tonight will likely bring a California red, so there will be plenty to drink. We'll use the good china, and three sets of glasses: for the prosecco, the red, and the sparkling water.

I wonder. Do I prefer planning a dinner to actually enjoying one? Thinking about food to actually eating it?

(4)

When I'm feeling particularly droopy at my desk, I often pop a piece of Ghost Chocolate. From Nobska Farms, on Cape Cod. We met the couple who run it at a market. It's all chili peppers for them. Hot sauces, jam, salsa. And they feed their chickens peppers too. Their eggs are creamier, the yolks a deeper orange than any I have ever eaten. And they invented this spicy chocolate made with mango, pumpkin seeds, and ghost peppers. Packs a punch. The two people are charming. Like us, they're semi-geezers, and the farm is their second career. I told them they should market their chocolate as a weight-loss item. It's so good, and so hot, that you can only eat a small amount. The man laughed and said, "Self-limiting."

(5)

The "ancienne" baguette from Clear Flour, made from both wheat and rye, is no longer as crisp as it was when we ate half of it with dinner. It's soft but has a nice chew, and it's tasty. I rip off a chunk, slop some blueberry jam on it, and wolf it down. Then I have another. The granite counter is soon littered with crumbs and drips of jam. It's after midnight and, as almost always at this hour, I'm having the first of my nighttime snacks. My routine is pretty consistent. I wake up after an hour or two of sleep, and I'm craving food, but I can't be really hungry since I had a big meal just a few hours ago. But I feel voracious, and my stomach demands gratification. It's bad to eat so late, I know. I could force myself not to eat, but then, or so I calculate, it would be more difficult to get back to sleep, which is what I need most. I'm not too heavy, but I do carry some useless pounds, and I usually feel crappy, and with no appetite for breakfast, in the mornings. To wake up and not want to eat: how sad is that! Eggs sizzling in butter, pancakes on the grill, bacon, toast, potatoes, delicious morning buns—these attract me not at all.

When I'm done with my snack, I wipe off the counter. Then I brush my teeth and go back to bed. But not the one I share with Gina. In the middle of the night it's easier for me to fall sleep alone, so I go to either the couch in the living room or the guest bed in the study. By many a morning, I will have slept in three different places.

As a child in school, I would stare at the clock in agony, painfully waiting for the three o'clock bell that signaled release, and then I'd run outside, find a ball game of some sort, and then keep playing until I had to go home for dinner. These days, although there's precious little play left in me, my routine isn't so different. I struggle to stay in my office until late afternoon, and then flee to the gym to find, if not fun, at least some exercise, some cleansing, kinetic therapy.

During the long New England winters when it's dark well before five, and often cold and wet, we eat early, usually done by seven. Then I get stuck in front of the television or with a book I can barely read, and I'm bored and restless, and then I eat and then eat some more—most likely to alleviate the tension that comes with being cooped up. I understand why so many people turn to large doses of alcohol and drugs. I turn to small doses.

(6)

Last night it was salmon, the no-brainer fish, on the grill. It was all Cindy had left. Some rice and an Atlas Farms salad. We had to eat quickly in order to make it to the seven o'clock movie. But it was warm, and so at least we ate outdoors. Tonight will be the leftover rice. Start with scallions and ginger in the peanut oil, throw in asparagus, finely chopped carrots, some frozen pineapple. Then two eggs, pre-scrambled, with some fish sauce. Then throw in the cold rice. Douse with more fish sauce, maybe some hot as well. We have to leave by 6:40, so it will be quick and dirty. But not too bad.

(7)

Cooking, for me, is no fine art. Instead, it is little more than fresh ingredients and timing. But I was off on my pasta last night. Sausages out of their casings and into hot oil with garlic and a pinch of habanero. Then radicchio and arugula, early crops from the market. Some parmigiano and finishing oil at the end. But I put the radicchio and arugula into the pan way too early. After a couple of minutes, they were almost completely subsumed by the sausages. It all tasted pretty good, but it was mostly just the meat.

(8)

The clams in the linguine came from San Rossore, only a few miles away. Tiny and difficult to remove from their shells, but there were a lot of them, and they had flavored the pasta very well. The herring (in pesto!) was surprising, mild, and rich. The rabbit was tender, the sauce a bit thick. Gina's squid was succulent, her tuna only okay. Typical Tuscan bread (dry, no salt). A couple of bottles of local wine. A long dinner at Artilaufo, an old restaurant in Pisa, mid-June in a walled garden; the air was warm. We were with our friends Alfredo and Alessandra, who know the owners well.

No dinners like this in Boston, and not just because of the food. The gracious ease of it all. We've gone to this lovely place at least once during every one of our many trips here. The food is always good, sometimes excellent. It's comfortable, almost elegant, and nothing is pretentious. Like so many places in Pisa, it's a family operation, and it doesn't change much from year to year. The man, who does not speak English, at the tables, the woman in the kitchen.

I eat differently when I'm in Pisa. Instead of crude, day-and-night snacking, and dinners when I cannot stop myself from taking more even though I'm full, here it's only a coffee and pastry for breakfast; a bowl of pasta, some bread, and sparkling water for lunch; and something delicious for dinner. The portions are smaller than what I'm accustomed to, but more satisfying. At home I eat so often because I'm so restless. Here I eat when I'm hungry. And more slowly. The food is wonderful, the places where we're eating it, often outside, welcoming. It's enough, and I easily go through the rest of the day, my stomach at peace. At home I wolf down a sandwich while at my desk for lunch, and then it's back to the struggle to stay alert, to read, to write, to do something worthwhile. My ordinary life is infused with subtle pressure and reprimand. Do not eat more of the chocolate always available in my desk. Do not check the website of the Boston Red Sox or the *New York Times*. Do not smoke more than three cigarettes a day or eat bread and leftovers at three in the morning. But I do all of these things, over and over, and my consciousness of having done them, and then of having to pay penance by going to the gym, is never quite absent.

Except in Pisa, where the pressure dissipates, and my body changes. The burden on my digestive system lightens. I lose weight. I am not called to the bathroom nearly as frequently. I sleep better. At home, I awaken every hour or two. Here I can stay in bed for as many as four. This, plus Alfredo and Alessandra, who are not only great friends but also wonderful cooks, and at whose home we eat often, might be reason enough to move to this place.

(9)

Lunch was tagliatelle with black truffles. The flavor was impressive, but the pasta was cold. And we were overcharged. This was not too surprising, because we were in Florence, a town I usually avoid. But Alessandra had recommended two recently renovated museums, and so we decided to go. As usual, she was right. The Museo dell' Opera del Duomo has a gorgeous collection of works originally created for the Florence Cathedral. The Ospedale dei Innocenti, an orphanage that operated from the fifteenth to the nineteenth century, now houses a sizable collection of Renaissance art. Both were splendid, and neither was crowded, which for me is always a plus, nearly a need.

The day was long and tiring. We slept on the train back to Pisa and had no energy when we returned. So we just bought some bread and finished up the gorgonzola dolce and a bottle of Sagrantino. We ate in the garden of our small inn. Our energy restored, we managed to walk to De'Coltelli for gelato. Sitting on the wall on the banks of the Arno, watching the lively, endlessly discursive clusters of young Italians, we enjoyed our chocolate and lime-ginger. Bursting with flavor and freshness, it's better than American ice cream. We're convinced De'Coltelli is the best in town, but this view is not universally shared by the locals.

(10)

Giovanni and Francesco, the two teenage sons of Alfredo and Alessandra, took us to their favorite sandwich shop for lunch. Well, it isn't really much a shop, just a kitchen with a counter that opens to the street in front of it. A one-man show, and his name is Marco. He makes sandwiches. Pork and beef, grilled lightly, accompanied by his sauces and some arugula. I enjoy hearing the boys talk with Marco, even if I can understand only bits of their conversation. Like their parents, they take their food seriously. They ask him questions, specify precisely what they want, and despite the fact that there's a line, he takes his time discussing their sandwich. We buy a couple of bottles of water from a convenience store, then find seats in the piazza to eat. Lovely boys, good food.

(11)

For decades, I (like most Americans in those days) didn't think much about food. I always ate plenty, and I didn't hate to cook, but that was about it. I went only to the least expensive restaurants. I was not much of a drinker, so I wasn't able to discern significant differences between various kinds of wine or beer.

For decades, I didn't think much about the *Odyssey*. Even as a kid, I wasn't much taken by the adventures of Books IX–XII. They seemed silly. As I got older, I became an *Iliad* guy, which I thought was the far deeper of the two epics. After all, its characters face death on the battlefield on a regular basis. The *Odyssey*, by contrast, is remarkably domestic. Its hero just wants to go home, and in almost every chapter a meal of some sort is described in loving detail.

Much has changed in the past twenty years or so. I now spend an inordinate amount of time planning meals, then shopping for, making, and serving food. I feel smaller if I'm not doing these things. I enjoy going to good restaurants, drinking fine wine and beer. And the *Odyssey* now seems deeper than the *Iliad*.

2

Dionysus

I Euripides' *Bacchae*

Wine is a sure presence at a Homeric supper, and its effects, especially inducing sweet sleep, are mentioned regularly. So too are libations poured at every sacrifice. Still, food, not drink, commands a greater share of the poet's attention. In fact, when Homer does explicitly address wine, he usually underscores its negatives. So, for example, a member of Odysseus' own crew, poor dumb Elpenor, "fell asleep with wine" (X.614) and then tumbled off a roof and broke his neck. And then there's the story of Eurytion, a centaur, who crashed a wedding party, got drunk, and then wreaked havoc.

> Here is the evil wine can do
> to those who swig it down. Even the centaur
> Eurytion, in Peiríthoös' hall
> among the Lapíthai, came to a bloody end
> because of wine; wine ruined him: it crazed him,
> drove him wild for rape in that great house.
> The princes cornered him in fury, leaping on him
> to drag him out and crop his ears and nose.
> Drink had destroyed his mind.
>
> XXI.330–9

As a centaur, a hybrid of horse and man, Eurytion, like Polyphêmos, is uncivilized. He lacks the knowledge that properly socialized people have: namely, how to drink well. And this means doing so at dinner, in order to loosen the tongue so that stories may be freely shared. Odysseus, of course, understands this well.

> "Listen," he said,
> "Eumaios, and you others, here's a wishful
> tale that I shall tell. The wine's behind it,

vaporing wine, that makes a serious man
break down and sing, kick up his heels and clown,
or tell some story that were best untold."

                                                    XIV.545–51

In general, however, wine is largely kept quiet in the *Odyssey*. For this reason, in the previous chapter only one paltry sentence directly addressed it. "Since a Homeric supper is never without wine, [Meneláos] calls his guests to the table not only to eat, but also to take the edge off with drink." But what edge is this, and why does wine make it go away? The answers require a discussion of Dionysus, the god of the vine and its intoxicating fruit. He is barely mentioned by Homer, and so we turn next to Euripides' great play, *The Bacchae*, where he is the central, indeed the overwhelming, figure.[1]

It begins with a speech from Dionysus himself. After much sojourning in the east, he has returned to his birthplace: the Greek city of Thebes. His birth was, even by mythological standards, spectacular. Zeus, as he was wont to do, had sex with Semele, a mortal woman, the daughter of Cadmus, legendary king of Thebes. Since a god's intercourse invariably bears fruit, she got pregnant. Hera, Zeus' wife—and the protector of marriage, and thus of social convention—got wind of the event. Disguised as a mortal woman, she became Semele's friend and planted in her a seed of doubt: was her secret lover really a god? She advised Semele to beg Zeus to reveal himself fully to her. He reluctantly agreed, and then, in a rather perverse display of his integrity, he blasted her with his thunderbolt. Semele was incinerated, but Zeus rescued the fetus and sewed it into his own thigh, from which Dionysus was born or, to be more accurate, reborn. For he is just that: the god twice-born from both a mother and a father's "male womb" (527). He is double-sided, bipolar, from the start.

Dionysus has returned to Thebes in order to "refute that slander spoken by my mother's sisters" (26). They had been spreading the false rumor that Semele's lover, Dionysus' father, was actually a mortal, and that Cadmus invented the story of his daughter's relationship with Zeus in order to protect the family's good name. On their telling, Zeus blasted Semele only because Cadmus lied about him. Dionysus is determined to avenge this defamation of his parentage and to be recognized for what he truly is: a god.

This is the first lesson in Dionysian wisdom. The god—alien, intrusive, subversive, and demanding—enters from outside and is then resisted by those who fear his power. But resistance inevitably proves both futile and disastrously wrongheaded.

In the *Bacchae*, the opposition to Dionysus comes from Pentheus. The son of Agave, one of Semele's sisters, he too is the grandson of Cadmus, and so he and Dionysus are cousins. Now the young king of Thebes, he occupies the throne his grandfather had abdicated. And so Dionysus' wrath is directed at Pentheus, about whom he bitterly complains:

> Who now revolts against divinity *in me*;
> thrusts *me* from his offerings; forgets *my* name
> in his prayers. Therefore I shall *prove* to him
> and every man in Thebes that I am god.

44–8

Dionysus has arrived to receive his due recognition, exact revenge, "vindicate [his] mother Semele" (41), and assert himself into the pantheon of Greek gods. He has invaded Thebes. And his first victims are women.

> I have stung them with frenzy, hounded them from home
> up to the mountains where they wander, crazed of mind,
> and compelled to wear my orgies' livery.
> Every woman in Thebes—but the women only—
> I drove from home mad.

33–9

The women of Thebes, typically confined to the home where they are subordinated to their men, have been transformed into Bacchae or Maenads, frenzied female devotees of Dionysus, the god of mad liberation. He has inspired them to abandon their proper duties as managers of the domestic sphere. No longer are they caring for children, cooking, or weaving wool. For this is precisely the havoc Dionysus wreaks: he overthrows established order, hierarchy, and the sense of responsibility that keeps people reliably stationed in their social roles. He empowers the women to escape the oppressive sobriety of their quotidian lives and to flee to the mountains where flora and fauna, and they themselves, run wild.

This is the edge Dionysus takes off. He obliterates the boundaries, inhibitions, and norms that govern—indeed, make possible—ordinary life. The female chorus, calling him by one of his several names, "Bromius," sings his praises:

> He is sweet upon the mountains. He drops to the earth
> from the running packs.
> He wears the holy fawn-skin. He hunts the wild goat
> and kills it.

He delights in the raw flesh.
He runs to the mountains of Phrygia, to the mountains
of Lydia he runs!
He is Bromius who leads us! *Evohé*!

With milk the earth flows! It flows with wine!
It runs with the nectar of bees!

Like frankincense in its fragrance
is the blaze of the torch he bears.
Flames float out from his trailing wand
        as he runs, as he dances,
        kindling the stragglers,
        spurring with cries,
And his long curls stream to the wind!

And he cries, as they cry, *Evohé*—
        On, Bacchae!
        On, Bacchae!
Follow, glory of golden Tmolus,
        hymning god
        with a rumble of drums,
with a cry, *Evohé*! to the Evian god,
with a cry of Phrygian cries,
when the holy flute like honey plays
the sacred song of those who go
to the mountain! to the mountain!

135–65

Dionysus, or one of his avatars, draped in an animal's hide, seizes a wild goat, tears it to pieces, and then eats the flesh raw. He runs upon the ground flowing with milk, honey, and wine. Torches blaze, drums roar, the shrill notes of the flute shrieks, wild joy prevails. The women, the Bacchae, feel astonishingly alive. For Dionysus is far more than the god of wine. His domain is pulsating life itself. As E. R. Dodds memorably put it, Dionysus

is ... the Power in the tree ... the blossoming ... the fruit-bringer ... the abundance of life. His domain is ... the whole of [liquid nature]—not only the liquid fire in the grape, but the sap thrusting in a young tree, the blood pounding in the veins of a young animal, all the mysterious and uncontrollable tides that ebb and flow in the life of nature.[2]

And his crowning glory is fermentation, the metabolic process by which the sugars in decaying fruit are converted to alcohol, by which the elixir of life comes from death. "It was fermentation," Lawrence Osborne writes, "that made [the Greeks] think of the indestructibility of [life]. As things decay, they give off enigmatic life; they bubble and seethe and self-transform."[3]

With his gorgeous long and curly hair—which, to the severe eyes of Pentheus, is offensively effeminate—Dionysus spurs the women to join in celebration. He induces an intoxication that dissolves the edge, the inhibitions on which society itself depends.

All this may seem attractive and, yes, there is a palpable sense of joy as the women, even old ones, feel their feet flying off the ground. But their celebration is also ominous. The blood of the torn goat flows, the candles burn with flames that illuminate but also incinerate. Yes, it's good to drink wine, the Bacchae tell us, but do not deceive yourselves. This is no innocent pleasure.

Pentheus is appalled when he learns that the women of his city, including his mother and aunts, are missing, and hears the rumors of their mountain doings.

> I happened to be away out of the city,
> but reports reached me of some strange mischief here,
> stories of our women leaving home to frisk
> in mock ecstasies among the thickets on the mountain,
> dancing in honor of the latest divinity,
> a certain Dionysus, whoever he may be!
> In their midst stand bowls brimming with wine.
> And then one by one the women wander off
> to hidden nooks where they serve the lusts of men.
> Priestesses of Bacchus they claim they are,
> but it's really Aphrodite they adore.
>
> 215–24

His description of the women, whose Dionysian activities he himself has never witnessed, is strikingly inaccurate. Later in the play, a shepherd who actually had seen them explains that there were no men up there in the mountains, and the women were not worshipping Aphrodite—which is to say, they were not having sex. Instead, they were celebrating,

> modestly and soberly, not, as you think,
> drunk with wine, nor wandering, led astray
> by the music of the flute, to hunt their Aphrodite
> through the woods.
>
> 684–8

Pentheus' mistaken impression tells much. A self-righteous and ambitious young man, an aspiring ruler animated by a machismo unsupported by experience, he is certain the women are engaged in sexual misadventure. Clearly, he is projecting his own (repressed) sexual preoccupations onto the scene he imagines taking place in the mountains. Flush with pride at his newly attained political power, he is determined to bring the intoxicated madness to a halt.

> I am told a foreigner has come to Thebes
> from Lydia, one of those charlatan magicians,
> with long yellow curls smelling of perfumes,
> with flushed cheeks and the spells of Aphrodite
> in his eyes. His days and nights he spends
> with women and girls, dangling before them the joys
> of initiation in his mysteries.
> But let me bring him underneath that roof
> and I'll stop his pounding with his wand and tossing
> his head. But god, I'll have his head cut off!
>
> 229–41

Pentheus imagines Dionysus as an effeminate sex maniac, his cheeks aflame with a post-coital glow the young king himself has never experienced. He is desperate to stop the god's "pounding with his wand" by cutting off his head. The symbolism is obvious. Pentheus' aggression is fueled by his severely repressed sexual urges.

Cadmus begs his grandson to drop his violent machinations. Together with Teiresias, the blind prophet of Thebes, he has become, weirdly enough, a devotee of Dionysus. (This is why he abdicated the throne.) The two old men want to dance with the Maenads and forget they are old. Teiresias tries to talk sense into Pentheus.

>   Mark my words,
> Pentheus. Do not be so certain that power
> is what matters in the life of man; do not mistake
> for wisdom the fantasies of your sick mind.
> Welcome the god to Thebes; crown your head;
> pour him libations and join his revels.
>
> 309–14

Consumed by anger, plagued by unconscious desire and envy, Pentheus is deaf to his imprecations. His young, masculine mind is sick indeed, and so he orders his soldiers to do the impossible: to capture and domesticate Dionysus.

As for the rest of you, go and scour the city
for that effeminate stranger, the man who infects our women
with this strange disease and pollutes our beds.
And when you take him, clap him in chains
and march him. He shall die as he deserves—
by being stoned to death. He shall come to rue
his merrymaking here in Thebes.

351–8

Teiresias is mortified by Pentheus' crusade against the god.

Reckless fool,
you do not know the consequences of your words.
You talked madness before, but this is raving
lunacy!

359–63

"The words of fools," Teiresias says, "finish in folly" (369). Resisting madness
is its own kind of madness, for Dionysus is overwhelming. He is a god. The
chorus reiterates the warning.

To rich and poor [Dionysus] gives
the simple gift of wine,
the gladness of the grape.
But him who scoffs he hates.

422–6

Pentheus' stupid masculinity, repressed sexuality, and teetotaling austerity
are hateful to Dionysus, the god "of banquets" (376). For nothing is wrong with
the simple gift of wine. After all, life is brutal because it is short: "Briefly we live.
Briefly,/ then die" (397). Dionysus' gifts—"laughter ... the flute ... the loosing of
cares ... sleep" (380–5)—offer a reprieve from the inevitable "unhappiness that
comes with mundaneness, with normal life, which after all—and without undue
exaggeration—leads to old age and death."[4] To hold intoxication in contempt
is to vastly overestimate the resources human beings have at their disposal.
It is a massive failure of self-knowledge. In the terms of Euripides' play, it is a
blasphemy, for it is to think oneself superior to, because without need of, a god.
The chorus, echoing sentiments that saturate the *Odyssey* as well, explains at
length:

Unwise are those who aspire,
who outrange the limits of man.

Briefly, we live. Briefly,
then die. Wherefore, I say,
he who hunts a glory, he who tracks
some boundless, superhuman dream,
may lose his harvest here and now
and garner death. Such men are mad,
their counsels evil.

394–403

In the *Odyssey*, the gods are foils who illuminate by contrast what we are: mortal beings with limited control over our too short lives. To think otherwise, which is precisely what Pentheus does, is catastrophic. Like many a young and privileged man, he revels in his lofty position and feels himself to be invulnerable. He "outranges" the limits of the human. Were he thinking straight, he would concentrate on his "harvest here and now." He would value his family and celebrate the simple, even pathetic, pleasures of domestic life. Instead, by trying to hunt down his mother and aunts, and by holding his grandfather's advice in utter contempt, he is tearing his household apart. He is, in the chorus's words, "mad." But be careful with this word, for the women who worship Dionysus are mad as well. Their madness, however, is sacral and a much needed, even therapeutic, interlude in their difficult lives.

Pentheus does manage to corral Dionysus, although of course he can do so only because the god is willing to play along. Dionysus is brought to the king with his hands tied. The two cousins finally meet.

So,

you *are* attractive, stranger, at least to women—
which explains, I think, your presence here in Thebes.
Your curls are long. You do not wrestle, I take it.
And what fair skin you have—you must take care of it—
no daylight complexion; no, it comes from the night
when you hunt Aphrodite with your beauty.

452–8

Pentheus is much taken with Dionysus' smooth, white skin—markedly in contrast to a Greek soldier-king who marches to battle in the hot sun—and he even wonders what sort of cream the god, who surely doesn't wrestle, might use. Again, erotic attraction, and sexual confusion, is the unmistakable undertone of his vitriol. He is, as the god so aptly says, "fed on his desires" (618).

Pentheus next does something truly terrible. He cuts Dionysus' hair, despite the god's warning: "My hair is holy./ My curls belong to god" (491). The young king chains him and throws him into a makeshift prison. In a voice perhaps tinged with some sadness, Dionysus explains to his cousin the awful mistake he is making:

> You do not know
> the limits of your strength. You do not know
> what you do. You do not know who you are.
>
> 505–8

To believe a human can imprison a god is a monumental failure of self-knowledge. We are weak and fragile beings who need help, from others and from external supplements, to get through the night. Dionysus, god of fermentation, offers it to us. To deny his gifts, to proudly declare oneself a teetotaler, is to believe oneself to be sufficient and, as the *Bacchae* is meant to teach its audience, we are surely not that. As Lawrence Osborne puts it, "It is only when you are surrounded by teetotalers that you realize how indebted you are to the chemistries of alcohol" (p. 81).

Dionysus, of course, easily escapes from prison. Drawing thunder and lightning down from the skies, he reduces Pentheus' palace to ashes, and then calmly joins his devotees. To them he recounts his actions:

> There I, in turn humiliated him, outrage for outrage.
> He seemed to think that he was chaining me but never once
> so much as touched my hands. He fed on his desires.
> Inside the stable he intended as my jail, instead of me,
> he found a bull and tried to rope its knees and hooves.
> He was panting desperately, biting his lips with his teeth,
> his whole body drenched with sweat, while I sat nearby
> quietly watching.
>
> 616–23

The two cousins are polar opposites. The god, an androgynous, Protean being who briefly takes on the form of a bull—an animal associated with both fertility and ferocity—is calm and confident, while the young king is fervid, bursting at the seams. "A man, a man, and nothing more,/ yet he presumed to wage a war with god" (636). Pentheus doesn't have a chance, and Dionysus knows it. The cousins square off, but before their argument can go very far, a shepherd arrives and interrupts the scene. He happened upon the Dionysian revels when he was grazing his flocks in the mountains and tells the king what he saw:

> Sir, I have seen
> the holy Maenads, the women who ran barefoot

and crazy from the city, and I wanted to report
to you and Thebes what weird fantastic things,
what miracles, and more than miracles,
these women do.

                                                                    664–9

Again reminding us that Pentheus was dead wrong in his (wishful) image of what the women were doing up in the mountains, he reports that, far from engaging in sexual orgies, they were behaving "modestly and soberly" (686). This is not to say, however, that their revels were innocent, or even intelligible.

First they let their hair fall loose, down
over their shoulders, and those whose straps had slipped
fastened their skins of fawn with writhing snakes
that licked their cheeks. Breasts swollen with milk,
new mothers who had left their babies behind at home
nestled gazelles and young wolves in their arms,
suckling them. Then they crowned their hair with leaves,
ivy and oak and flowering bryony. One woman
struck her thyrsus against a rock and a fountain
of cool water came bubbling up. Another drove
her fennel in the ground, and where it struck the earth,
at the touch of god, a spring of wine poured out.
Those who wanted milk scratched the soil
with bare fingers and the while milk came welling up.
Pure honey spurted, streaming, from their wands.

                                                                    694–711

A fantastic scene of fluid abundance and peaceful communion with nature. The women, typically so rigidly bound to their homes, have let their hair down and adorned it with vegetation. Their blouses, made not from the cloth they themselves are required to manufacture but from the hides of deer they have killed with their bare hands, are fastened with squirming snakes, which lick their cheeks. Young mothers have left babies at home and relieve their swollen breasts by suckling gazelles and wolves. Water bubbles up from rocks; milk, wine, and honey from the earth itself. Liquidity abounds, normal boundaries dissolve, for Dionysus is the god of the wet who threatens the pillars of the dry, of conventional order.

There is also a terribly dark side, as the shepherd reports. Eager to "earn a little favor with King Pentheus" (720), he had hoped to capture Agave and return her

to town. Hiding in the forest, he tried to ambush her, but the Bacchae detected
his presence before he could spring.

> With one voice they cried aloud:
> "*O Iacchus! Son of Zeus!*" "*O Bromius,*" they cried
> until the beasts and all the mountain seemed
> wild with divinity. And when they ran,
> everything ran with them.
>
> 724–8

A fantastic image: not just the women, but all the animals, maybe even the
sticks and stones, attacked the hapless man. He tells the tale:

> At this we fled
> and barely missed being torn to pieces by the women.
> Unarmed, they swooped down upon the herds of cattle
> grazing there on the green of the meadow. And then
> you could have seen a single woman with bare hands
> tear a fat calf, still bellowing with fright,
> in two, while others clawed the heifers to pieces.
>
> There were ribs and cloven hooves scattered everywhere,
> and scraps smeared with blood hung from the fir trees.
> And bulls, their raging fury gathered in their horns,
> lowered their heads to charge, then fell, stumbling
> to the earth, pulled down by hordes of women
> and stripped of flesh and skin more quickly, sire,
> than you could blink your royal eyes.
>
> 733–45

Next, the women swept down from the mountain and attacked an
unsuspecting village, whose men naturally took up their weapons in order to
resist. But Dionysus is irresistible.

> For the men's spears were pointed and sharp, and yet
> drew no blood, whereas the wands the women threw
> inflicted wounds. And then the men ran,
> routed by women.
>
> 761–5

Women routing men: Dionysus destroys the fortress of masculine hierarchy.
The result is both glorious—milk and honey flow—and terrifying—women tear

raging bulls to pieces. The shepherd, as he understands full well, was lucky to have escaped with his life. He counsels poor, doomed Pentheus:

> Whoever this god may be,
> sire, welcome him to Thebes. For he is great
> in many other ways as well. It was he,
> or so they say, who gave to mortal men
> the gift of lovely wine by which our suffering
> is stopped.

768–74

Teetotaling Pentheus, proud and erect, again ignores good advice. He orders his soldiers to attack. "I shall make a great slaughter in the woods of Cithaeron" (796), he boasts, his rage seemingly fueled by the prospect of killing women. Dionysus warns him, yet again, not to "take arms against a god" (788). Suddenly, though, the god has an apparent change of heart, and he offers what appears to be a lifeline to Pentheus. "Would you like to *see* their revels on the mountain?" (813), he asks. Pentheus can barely contain his enthusiasm, for, as Euripides has made clear all along, his violent impulses are leavened by lust. "I would pay a great sum to see that sight" (814), he quickly responds.

There is, however, a catch. Because, as the shepherd so vividly described, the Maenads are fiercely protective of the sanctity of their rites, Pentheus must dress as a woman. Of course, the proud boy protests: "What? You want *me*, a man, to wear a woman's dress? ... I *cannot* bring myself to dress in women's clothes" (835). Soon, however, he relents. In fact, he even seems to welcome the prospect of cross-dressing. He not only puts on a dress and a wig but, as the translator puts it, also luxuriates with some "coy primping" (925). Just as a wealthy woman might speak to her maid, Pentheus says to Dionysus, "I am in your hands completely" (933). Dress me as you will, just as long as I am pretty. Poor boy. So confused.

As is typical in a Greek tragedy, the ensuing violence is only described in words, while the action is kept off stage. A messenger tells the awful tale. Pentheus, nicely decked out, hid in a rock outcrop in order to spy upon the women. The scene he witnessed was peaceful, as they were doing no more than weaving wreaths of ivy and "frisking like fillies/ newly freed from the painted bridles" (1056). Pentheus wanted to get closer, to see more. Apparently to protect him, Dionysus placed him high up in a tree. In fact, it was an ambush. At that height Pentheus was fully, fatally exposed. "The Maenads saw him/ more clearly

than he saw them" (1075). And then, in the god's coup de grâce, he was called
out by Dionysus himself:

> "Women, I bring you the man who has mocked
> at you and me and at our holy mysteries.
> Take vengeance upon him." And as he spoke
> a flash of awful fire bound earth and heaven.
>
> 1079–84

An uncanny silence descended. But soon the women, activated in rage, begin
pelting the tree with sticks and stones. Pentheus' tree was, however, too high,
and so they missed their mark. Then they, led by Agave, Pentheus' own mother,
tore the tree down: "Thousands of hands/ tore the fir tree from the earth, and
down, down/ from his high perch fell Pentheus" (1110). Agave was the first to
reach him when he hit the ground. Pentheus flung off his wig and begged his
mother for recognition:

> *"No, no, Mother! I am Pentheus,*
> *your own son, the child you bore to Echion!*
> *Pity me, spare me, Mother! I have done a wrong,*
> *But do not kill your own son for my offense."*

> But she was foaming at the mouth, and her crazed eyes
> rolling with frenzy. She was mad, stark mad,
> possessed by Bacchus. Ignoring his cries of pity,
> she seized his left arm at the wrist; then, planting her
> foot upon his chest, she pulled, wrenching away
> the arm at the shoulder—not by her own strength,
> for the god had put inhuman power in her hands.
> Ino, meanwhile, on the other side was scratching off
> his flesh. Then Autonoë and the whole horde
> of Bacchae swarmed upon him. Shouts everywhere,
> he screaming with what little breath was left,
> they shrieking in triumph. One tore off an arm,
> another a foot still warm in its shoes. His ribs
> were clawed clean of flesh and every hand
> was smeared with blood as they played ball with scraps
> of Pentheus' body.
>
> 1118–37

Dwell on the details, if you can bear it. The unimaginable violence is
sickeningly compounded by the fact that the perpetrators included the boy's

own mother and aunts. Most shockingly, Agave takes her son's severed head and impales it upon her stick, which she raises in mad triumph.

Dionysus gives us the gift of sweet wine by which our sufferings, so definitive of ordinary life, are alleviated. But he is the bipolar god. Intoxication can be sweet, and help us ward off the sleeplessness of dark night, but it also causes us to act in ways we would never, ever do while sober. Dionysus is the twice-born god of both joy and horror, insight and madness, innocence and unspeakable violence.

The action on stage resumes when Cadmus, carrying what remains of his grandson's shattered body, which he had "painfully assembled from Cithaeron's glens" (1118), appears. Agave, still in the grip of Dionysian madness, proudly presents her father with what she "seems to think is some mountain lion's head which she carries in triumph" (1140). Naturally, Cadmus, who is sober, is mortified.

> This is a grief
> so great it knows no size. I cannot look.
> *This* is the awful murder your hands have done.
>
> 1243–7

Best for Agave to have died on the spot. But the god inflicts upon her an even worse punishment: sobriety. When she awakens from her madness, she realizes what she has done. And then she is utterly ruined. "No! O gods, I see the greatest grief there is" (1283). Like many a drunk, she does not remember much of what happened the night before. "But *we*, what were we doing on the mountain?" (1293), she pitifully asks. And then she learns the horrifying truth. She had denied that Dionysus, her own nephew, "was truly a god" (1296), and so was punished beyond belief.

II The Dionysian Journey of Lawrence Osborne

What to make of Euripides' *Bacchae*? More specifically, what does it actually mean to worship Dionysus, to affirm his divinity? Perhaps a short detour will help. It will be led by a writer (already quoted) whose understanding of the Dionysian runs deep: Lawrence Osborne. A journalist, novelist, and an alcoholic, he embarked upon a two-year "cultural adventure" during which he travelled in Muslim countries. His goal: to explore societies whose desire was to extinguish men like himself. The selling of alcohol to Muslims has, for example, been banned in Pakistan since 1977, and so naturally Osborne decided to go there first. "In one of the most dangerous and alcohol-hostile countries in the world, I wondered what it would be like to intoxicate oneself" (p. 106). His book *The Wet and the Dry* not only recounts his travels, but along the way it offers penetrating observations about cultures that, like Pentheus, resist the Dionysian.

(Please note: Osborne is not a scholar of Islam. As a result, several of his statements are exaggerated, overly general, and perhaps offensive. He does not, for example, clearly distinguish Islamic extremism from the religion in general. This section is not meant to endorse his views, nor does it purport to offer any serious commentary about, and certainly no critique of, Islam. Instead, its goal is only to pry open the mind of a Dionysian and try to understand what he worships and why.)

Throughout his journey, Osborne was fascinated by true believers. He met several in the Indonesian town of Solo, a hotbed of Islamic extremism. There he had conversations with serious young men, about the same age as Pentheus, who were students in religious schools. In response to his asking why they condemned alcohol so severely, one explained, "The terrible thing about drink ... was that it took one out of one's normal consciousness" (p. 8). Another, a boy who hoped to study in Saudi Arabia, said this: "Alcohol was forbidden by Islam because under its influence we are not 'true to ourselves or our relationships'" (p. 153).

On the one hand, Osborne knows the boys in Solo are right. We are not normal, responsible, or duty-bound when we are drunk. Sober, we monitor ourselves and stay vigilant lest we do something wrong or say something stupid. We are self-conscious. Sober, we fear the judgments of others, see ourselves through their eyes, and put a clamp on our impulses in order to stay straight. Such inhibitions may keep us safe (for a while), but they also keep us from merging with the gyrating bodies on the dance floor. They lock us into ordinary life, as we do little more than prepare for a future, "which after all—and without undue exaggeration—leads to old age and death" (p. 141).

By the most vivid contrast, the drinker "knows that life is not mental and not a matter of control and demarcation" (p. 86). He "is a Dionysiac, a dancer who sits still, a mocker. He doesn't need your seriousness or your regard" (p. 65). He sheds his fears and inhibitions, and his obligations, by partaking of the god's great gift: fermentation, which "excites and fills one with optimism and lust" (p. 28). "It was fermentation," Osborne writes, "that made [the Greeks] think of the indestructibility of [life]. As things decay, they give off enigmatic life; they bubble and seethe and self-transform" (p. 67). Thanks to Dionysus, we too can, on rare occasions, bubble without worrying where we have to go next or what other people think.

One of Osborne's more striking and controversial (and perhaps even offensive) suggestions is that in countries like Pakistan, Saudi Arabia, and even Egypt and Lebanon—places where "the god of the desert is now in the ascendant once again" (p. 27)—the prohibition of alcohol, of the wet, goes hand in glove with the oppression of women. As he puts it, "the suppression of alcohol is itself a sexual suppression" (p. 79), and so he dares to speak of the "misogyny of the Teetotaler God" (p. 80). Even more broadly, this hot and dry god puts a clamp on the very notion of freedom itself. By contrast, at least according to Osborne, the Greek veneration of Dionysus went hand in glove with its affirmation of democracy. It is no accident, he argues, that "the bar began as the coffee shop and café in eighteenth-century London and Paris," the two cities "where modern politics" (p. 32), and its declaration of human rights, began.

For all these reasons, to the Islamic extremists, alcohol is

> a symbol of the West, a tool of Satan that denatures the true believer; it is also associated with sexual laxity, the mingling of men and women, and one might say the bar itself—a free public space quite distinct from the mosque or the bazaar, the forms of public space that Muslim cities otherwise accommodate. Islamic radicals are right to hate and fear it. In bars, people leave their inhibitions behind.
>
> p. 116

Little surprise to him, then, that some of the most murderous of terrorist bombings, such as those in Bali in 2002 and 2005, have been of bars, places "in which a free society can conduct its informal business" (p. 128). About Solo, the hometown of the young men who detonated the bombs in Bali, he says this: "Six hundred thousand people, I kept thinking, and not a single bar. It seemed like a recipe for madness" (p. 9). Such madness, like Pentheus', is born from the rejection of the Dionysian, by the refusal to acknowledge that intoxication and the occasional obliteration of conventional boundaries is both necessary and good. It is a madness born from the hatred and fear of madness.

For Osborne, the prohibition of alcohol is ultimately unsustainable. He describes a town in Thailand, a largely Buddhist country, near the border with Islamic Malaysia. At home, the Malaysians cannot buy alcohol, and so they simply cross over in order to drink. Their thirst is unquenchable. "Perhaps," Osborne speculates, "every Muslim or Christian teetotaler dreams of a drink at the end of the rainbow." He actually hopes so, for he longs to find a Muslim alcoholic, a prospect which "gives me hope that the human race can be saved" (p. 8). Resistance to Dionysus, as the *Bacchae* so powerfully depicts, invariably proves not only futile but also self-destructive. For Dionysus is real. He represents a fundamental feature of human life, and so the attempt to repress him, as Pentheus learned too late, is a massive failure of self-knowledge. For we are mortal. Irretrievable loss is our lot, and suffering is in our future. And so we should be grateful to Dionysus, who grants us a reprieve and lets us run, however briefly, free.

Like Euripides, though, Osborne refuses to avert his gaze from the destructive side of Dionysus, the bipolar god. He understands that some people, like his former father-in-law, drink themselves to death. Nonetheless, to them he says, chillingly, "You go right ahead because you are human and drink is sweet" (p. 1). Having experienced his own struggles with addiction, he knows its consequences can be hellish. But it is, he says in a voice chastened by decades of hard drinking, a "vital hell" (p. 131).

> The reasons for hating [alcohol] are all valid. But by the same token they are not really reasons at all. For in the end alcohol is merely us, a materialization of our own nature. To repress it is to repress something that we know about ourselves but cannot celebrate or even accept.
>
> p. 225

III William James as a Dionysian

A second detour will be led by William James, who, even if he never uses the word, is another Dionysian. His book, *The Varieties of Religious Experience*, analyzes the different ways in which human beings encounter, and have their lives transformed by, the divine.[5] Whether these experiences accurately correspond to an external or objective reality—whether, for example, God actually exists or not—is not James's question. He is no theologian. Instead, "religious feelings and religious impulses must be [my] subject, and I must confine myself to those more developed subjective phenomena recorded in literature" (p. 12). Ignoring "the institutional branch" of religion entirely, he focuses on "the feelings, acts, and experiences of individual men in their solitude, so far as they apprehend themselves to stand in relation to whatever they may consider the divine" (p. 32). *Varieties* is a book written by a psychologist who is convinced that "the religious propensities of man must be at least as interesting as any other of the facts pertaining to his mental constitution" (p. 12).

James finds one feature to be present in virtually all of his case studies.

> For common men "religion" ... signifies always a *serious* state of mind. If any
> one phrase could gather its universal message, that phrase would be, "All is *not*
> vanity in this Universe, whatever the appearances may suggest." ... [Religion]
> says "hush" to all vain chatter and smart wit.
>
> p. 37

The religious encounter promises that all is not "vanity" (from the Latin *vanus*, "empty"). Instead, the world is full ... of substance, meaning, value. For there is "an unseen order" behind the appearances to which "our supreme good lies in harmoniously adjusting ourselves" (p. 48).

It may be difficult to maintain such a conviction, precisely because the "appearances" (ordinary experiences) are so often terribly demoralizing. Everything we see and touch, our finest achievements and all we hold dear, seems to pass away into nothingness. And so despair is a permanent human possibility—even, one might suppose, a reasonable response to our transience. If nothing lasts, then nothing matters; so why bother to get out of bed in the morning? No doubt, a vast number of human beings have asked just such a question. James, who suffered from depression as a young man, certainly did.

> The sanest and best of us are of one clay with lunatics and prison inmates, and
> death finally runs the robustest of us down. And whenever we feel this, such a
> sense of the vanity and provisionality of our voluntary career comes over us that
> all our morality appears but as a plaster hiding a sore it can never cure.
>
> p. 44

But despair is not the only option. In the *Odyssey*, it was Helen who reminded us of this. Her guests were weeping miserably as they shared recollections of the losses suffered in the Trojan War, and so she offered them a fine meal accompanied by wine, and the occasion to tell stories. For James, the great medicine is religion.

> Religion comes to our rescue. ... Like love, like wrath, like hope, ambition,
> jealousy, like every other instinctive eagerness and impulse, it adds to life an
> enchantment.
>
> p. 44

To reiterate: even if this statement is true, it hardly follows that religious experience is warranted by objective or external facts. Perhaps, as contemporary psychologists so regularly (and with such palpable glee) tell us, human beings systematically delude themselves. Perhaps the belief in an unseen and life-giving order is no more than a desperate kind of wish projection. Even so, religious experience would nevertheless have its own kind of integrity. For it is, James says, of "vital importance as a human faculty" (p. 47). In other words, it simply is part of who we are, whether God exists or not. No wonder, then, that the subtitle of James's book is *A Study of Human Nature*.

But why call James a Dionysian? It is because of what he says about the "mystical," which he identifies as the germ of all religious experience, and to which he devotes the "vital chapter" (p. 290) of his book.

The sensation of direct and immediate contact, or even merger, with the oneness of the universe is what characterizes the mystical experience. In its grip, "all the usual barriers between the individual and the Absolute" (p. 320) are overcome, and "elevation, elation and joyousness" (p. 304) replace the desiccating isolation of the everyday. According to James, of critical importance is the fact that the mystical experience is "ineffable"; it cannot be communicated by language. "The incommunicableness of the transport is the key note of all mysticism. Mystical truth exists for the individual who has the transport, but for no one else" (p. 309).

Ordinary language is inadequate to the task of faithfully expressing "cosmic consciousness," the feeling of being in unity with all things, for one simple reason. It is bound to the domain of multiplicity. A language is composed of many different words that are combined and regulated by a strict set of (syntactical) rules. It cannot, therefore, genuinely bespeak the one. Consider this simple example: "All is one." If this sentence is true, then it seems to provide evidence against itself. After all, it contains three words. Mystical "transport," in which unity overpowers multiplicity, is ineffable for just this reason.

In a parallel fashion, the mystical entails a rupture with "normal waking consciousness" (p. 296), which, like ordinary language, is essentially characterized by multiplicity and difference. I am aware that I am not you, you are not me, and neither of us is the tree or the dog. By contrast, mystical consciousness submerges such distinctions into the oneness of all things.

For better or worse, alcohol is frequently the trigger of the mystical experience.

The sway of alcohol over mankind is unquestionably due to its power to stimulate the mystical faculties of human nature, usually crushed to earth by the cold facts and dry criticism of the sober hour. Sobriety diminishes, discriminates, and says no; drunkenness expands, unites, and says yes. It is in fact the great exciter of the *Yes* function in man. It brings its votary from the chill periphery of things to the radiant core. It makes him for the moment one with truth. Not through mere perversity do men run after it. To the poor and unlettered it stands in the place of symphony concerts and of literature; and it is part of the deeper mystery and tragedy of life that whiffs and gleams of something that we immediately recognize as excellent should be vouchsafed to so many of us only in the fleeting earlier phases of what in its totality is so degrading a poisoning. The drunken consciousness is one bit of the mystic consciousness, and our total opinion of it must find its place in our opinion of that larger whole.

p. 296

Drunk, inhibitions break down, isolation gives way to union, obligations are forgotten, and our mundane, sober load is lightened. Drunk, we heed the call to dance, even though we do not know how. Bodies merge, and a feeling of unity with an unseen order, with life itself, envelops us. The *Yes* function kicks into gear. This is good and beautiful and, yes, I'm glad to be here.

We pass into mystical states from out of ordinary consciousness as from a less into a more, as from a smallness into a vastness, and at the same time as from an unrest to a rest. We feel them as unifying reconciling states. ... In them the unlimited absorbs the limits and peacefully closes the account.

p. 317

Alcohol, an organic solvent, dissolves the barriers separating individuals from each other and the world. It sparks the mystical, which in turn is the germ of all religious experience. Oddly enough, then, Dionysus, god of the vine and fermentation, can now be described as the god of religion itself.

James acknowledges that there is something pathetic about the human need for "so degrading a poison" as alcohol to generate mystical consciousness. Nonetheless, like Osborne, he does not condemn it. For he understands that we are feeble, frightened creatures, and without chemical assistance too many of us will be crushed by the demands of normal life and preoccupied by a future that finally leads only to death. He grants that there are other, more refined ways to open the doors of consciousness. Music, for example, can trigger feelings of harmony with the universe that ordinary language cannot. It can communicate "ontological messages which non-musical criticism is unable to contradict" (p. 321). In other words, it too can stimulate the mystical faculty, and without damaging the liver. Meditation and spiritual exercise, cultivated for centuries by practitioners of so many religions, offer nontoxic methods of achieving mystical union. But these are hard and hugely time-consuming, while intoxication is quick and easy and accessible to all, especially the "poor and unlettered," who need but take a drink.

Regardless of its chemical origin, James counts the experience alcohol generates as "excellent." And so he is fully in line with Euripides, who wrote, "To rich and poor [Dionysus] gives the simple gift of wine,/ the gladness of the grape."

What decisively certifies James as a Dionysian is his insistence that there is more to human life, to human consciousness, than rational thought.

> Our normal waking consciousness, rational consciousness as we call, is but one special type of consciousness, whilst all about it, parted from it by the filmiest of screens, there lie potential forms of consciousness entirely different. We may go through life without suspecting their existence; but apply the requisite stimulus, and at a touch they are there in all their completeness.
>
> p. 296

That human beings experience such altered states of consciousness— whether they are stimulated by alcohol or music or spiritual exercise—is, for James, a matter of psychological fact. However subjective or even delusional it may ultimately prove to be, the mystical experience is a component of human reality. It follows, therefore, that "no account of the universe in its totality can be final which leaves [it] … disregarded" (p. 296). Failure to learn this lesson was precisely what ruined Pentheus. He was all too sure he understood what was going on in the world, and how he, drawing only on his own resources as a king, could make it better. He disregarded, disrespected, Dionysus, and paid the terrible price. William James, by contrast, knows better. Even though he himself was largely a sober and serious-minded man, one who partook rarely if ever in actual Dionysian revelry, he understood that the boundaries demarcating his self and constituting his moral life were porous. He knew there was more, even if he himself had only the most fleeting experience of it. Consider this poignant little confession he offers: "Whether my treatment of mystical states will shed more light or darkness, I do not know, for my own constitution shuts me out from their enjoyment almost entirely, and I can speak of them only at second hand" (p. 290).

James wonders whether, given his thoroughly rational nature, he has missed something important. Nonetheless, he treats the mystical with the utmost respect. *The Varieties of Religious Experience*, then, is delicately balanced on a tightrope stretched between the mystical union of Dionysian merger and the analytical rigor of rational distance. Fittingly, then, its "vital chapter" concludes with the following question:

> It must always remain an open question whether mystical states may not possibly be such superior points of view, windows through which the mind looks

out upon a more extensive and inclusive world. ... They offer us hypotheses, hypotheses which we may voluntarily ignore, but which as thinkers we cannot possibly upset.

pp. 326–7

Such is the voice of, to risk a paradox, an intellectual Dionysian. Unlike Pentheus, James takes seriously the possibility that there is more to the world, to ourselves, than we think.

IV Nietzsche's *The Birth of Tragedy*

Alcohol is an organic solvent, and so it takes the edge off, providing a welcome, albeit dangerous, respite from the daily grind. By contrast, food keeps the edge on, for eating is the essential activity by which an animal maintains its form and thereby keeps itself separate from its immediate environment—keeps itself, in other words, alive. For this reason, eating is analogous to storytelling. The narrative impulse is to forge a sense of unity, of beginning, middle, and end, by ordering and embellishing a few items plucked from the storehouse of memory and projecting them toward an imagined future.

As Homer's *Odyssey* teaches so well, a good supper requires all three ingredients. They must, however, be kept in balance with one another in order to work their magic. The food needs to be good, but not so good that it commands all our attention. The wine needs to be ample, but not so ample that it renders us stupid or mute. The stories need to be told, but they should never be overly long or boring. Sadly, then, a good dinner party is hard to find.

Form maintenance and dissolution—the Greeks understood these two primal forces as both fundamental and complementary. And so they conceived of two gods to represent them: Apollo and Dionysus. The former, masculine and dry, is responsible for light, limits, symmetry, individuality, and geometry. As the god of vision he is ever distant, and so his weapon is the bow. The latter is affiliated with women and the wet, with intimacy, intoxication, immersion, wild music, and dance. Such, at least, was the view of Friedrich Nietzsche as he expressed it in his early work *The Birth of Tragedy*.[6]

For Nietzsche, the Apollinian impulse was brilliantly manifested in the clean lines of classical Greek sculpture and the luminous poetry of Homer. To illustrate the latter, consider the following passage (cited earlier). Odysseus and Penelope are on the verge of reunion, but he has not yet revealed his identity to her. Instead, he calls himself Aithon, a man who claims to know that her husband is still alive.

> Now all these lies he made appear so truthful
> she wept as she sat listening. The skin
> of her pale face grew moist the way pure snow
> softens and glistens on the mountains, thawed
> by Southwind after powdering from the West,
> and, as the snow melts, mountain streams run full:
> so her white cheeks were wetted by these tears
> shed for her lord—and he close by her side.
> Imagine how his heart ached for his lady,
> his wife in tears; and yet he never blinked;
> his eyes might have been made of horn or iron
> for all that she could see.
>
> *Odyssey*, XIX.240–50

Note the similes, the explicit comparisons of unlike things. Penelope's face is like a cold mountain glistening with snow. Just as a stream will gradually flow down its flank when the warm wind begins to melt its frozen surface, so too do tears run down her white cheeks when she hears Aithon's story of Odysseus. By contrast, Odysseus reveals none of his feelings. His eyes are like iron: dark, hard, and cold.

The elements of these similes are clear and distinct: cold mountain ... Penelope's face; snowy surface ... her white cheeks; Southwind ... Aithon's story; mountain stream ... her tears; iron ... Odysseus' eyes. In each pair, an inanimate and familiar object is invoked to describe something human. Homer's poetry is replete with vast numbers of just such images, and thus it has a remarkably visual, almost cinematic, character. And this is precisely what Nietzsche attributes to the Apollinian art impulse: it delights in the "pure contemplation of images" (p. 50). In turn, he associates these with dreams, for in these "we delight in the immediate understanding of figures" (p. 34). What he has in mind here is the extraordinary vividness of dreams. In sleep, with our senses quieted and distractions minimized, we can be consumed by the singular appearance of a dream image. This is why nightmares are so terrifying, and sexual dreams so stimulating.

> This joyous necessity of the dream experience has been embodied by the Greeks
> in their Apollo ... the god of all plastic energies ... the "shining one," the deity of
> light, is also ruler over the beautiful illusion of the inner world of fantasy.
>
> p. 35

Dream images may be dazzling, but they can also be confusing. A Homeric simile often has this effect as well. Consider the following passage. Demodokos, the blind bard of the Phaiákians, has just finished singing of the sack of Troy.

> And Odysseus
> let the bright molten tears run down his cheeks,
> weeping the way a wife mourns for her lord
> on the lost field where he has gone down fighting
> the day of wrath that came upon his children.
> At sight of the man panting and dying there,
> she slips down to enfold him, crying out;
> then feels the spears, prodding her back and shoulders,
> and goes bound into slavery and grief.
> Piteous weeping wears away her cheeks:
> but no more piteous than Odysseus's tears.
>
> VIII.560–71

Odysseus is compared to a woman who has just lost her husband in a battle. Just as she bends down to embrace his dead body, she herself is taken by enemy soldiers as war booty. The image clearly invokes a Trojan woman (perhaps Andromache, the wife of the great warrior Hektor, mercilessly slaughtered by Achilles). How strange: Odysseus, the victorious Greek warrior, compared to a defeated, humiliated woman soon to become a slave. It is not obvious why. And isn't this just the way dream images come to us as well? They may appear dazzlingly clear, but their meaning is not.

Nietzsche describes Apollo, the god of form, as the divine personification of the "*principium individuationis*" (p. 36), the principle of individuation. For he is responsible for the limits making it possible for an individual being to stand on its own. "For Apollo wants to grant repose to individual beings precisely by drawing boundaries between them, and by again and again calling them to mind as the most sacred laws of the world" (p. 72).

Nietzsche speculates that the Greeks, Homer in particular, became such geniuses of beautifully delineated Apollinian art precisely because they were so aware of its opposite: the liquid nature of the Dionysian, the oceanic flux sure to dissolve the boundaries keeping us intact. Their fears were succinctly expressed, he says, in the words of Silenus, a mythic hybrid of man and horse and, most important, the companion of Dionysus. His "terrible wisdom" (p. 45) was that human life, destined to sink under the waves and turn to nothing in the blink of an eye, is worthless, and so he proclaims, what is best for a human being is "not

to be born, not to be, to be *nothing*. But the second best for you is—to die soon"
(p. 42).[7]

If the Greeks were burdened by such a sensibility, they were also energized by
it. They may have felt "the terror and horror of existence," but they constructed
splendid defenses against it. In order to endure the wisdom of Silenus, the
Greeks "had to interpose between themselves and life the radiant dream-birth of
the Olympians" (p. 42). And this they did through Apollo and the "pleasurable
illusion" (p. 45) generated by his arts. In both sculpture and Homeric poetry,
the gods themselves—ageless, beautiful, never to be deformed—were present as
shining icons of the clean, dry stability we lack.

> The same impulse which calls art into being, as the complement and
> consummation of existence, seducing one to a continuation of life, was also
> the cause of the Olympian world which the Hellenic "will" made use of as a
> transfiguring mirror. Thus do the gods justify the life of man: they themselves
> live it—the only satisfactory theodicy! Existence under the bright sunshine of
> such gods is regarded as desirable in itself, and the real pain of Homeric men is
> caused by parting from it.
>
> p. 43

The last clause likely echoes the lament of Achilles in Hades. Recall the
scene: when Odysseus met him in the underworld, he expected the great warrior
to be content in his death. After all, Achilles had achieved the greatest prize
available to a hero: glory and living long in the memories of future generations.
And so he attempted to console his fallen comrade:

> But was there ever a man more blest by fortune
> than you, Akhilleus? Can there ever be?
> We ranked you with immortals in your lifetime,
> we Argives did, and here your power is royal
> among the dead men's shades. Think, then, Akhilleus:
> You need not be so pained by death.
>
> XI.569–75

But Achilles rebukes Odysseus sharply for his terrible misunderstanding.

> Let me hear no smooth talk
> of death from Odysseus, light of councils.
> Better, I say, to bread sod as a farm hand
> for some poor country man, on iron rations,
> than lord it over all the exhausted dead.
>
> XI.577–81

By his lights, no human accomplishment, neither great renown won on the battlefield nor stories told in generations to come, can make amends for the inevitable penalty of being alive: the dark and utter exhaustion of Hades. And so Achilles does not allow Odysseus to smooth-talk him out of despair. Even if others will sing our praises when we are gone, such songs, dead Achilles now understands, are no more than pathetic holding actions to ward off the nothingness, the formlessness, awaiting us all. His message is thus the Apollinian counterpoint to that of Silenus: "To die soon is worst of all ... the next worst—to die at all" (p. 43).

In response to their acute awareness of the impending threat of dissolution, the Greeks generated an antidote: shining images of Olympian gods in both word and marble, wonderful stories, beautiful art. But as Euripides' *Bacchae* so viscerally illustrates, the Greeks were too smart, and too confident, to avert their gaze from the "horror of existence," and so their arts included more than the dry lines of sculpture and the clean similes of Homeric epic. They also devised a kind of poetry inspired, not by Apollo, but by Dionysus, the god of the wet, of madness and dance: the lyric (from the Greek "lyre"), in which, as Nietzsche puts it, "language is strained to the utmost that it may imitate music" (p. 53). For music (as James understood) can express the Dionysian far better than ordinary language.

> Music stands in symbolic relation to the primordial contradiction and primordial pain in the heart of the primal unity, and therefore symbolizes a sphere which is beyond and prior to all phenomena ... hence *language*, as the organ and symbol of phenomena, can never by any means disclose the innermost heart of music.
>
> p. 55

This rather puzzling passage refers, perhaps, to the flow of time itself. Each moment both is and is not, for the present, the now, is but a gateway, with no duration of its own, through which the future slides into the past. It is both here and not-here at the same time. Such is the "primordial contradiction" at the heart of (temporal) reality. Such is the pain that comes with the realization that what-is is only because it will not be. More fundamental than all the many individuated, in-formed beings appearing in our ordinary lives—and appearing to be stable—is the oceanic flux sure to swamp us all. Dionysian music, an irresistible flow, gives better voice to this primal reality than ordinary language, whose fixed rules and distinct elements seem to promise stability. In another passage, from another book, Nietzsche expresses this thought more explicitly.

I see nothing other than becoming. Be not deceived. It is the fault of your myopia, not of the nature of things, if you believe you see land somewhere in the ocean of coming-to-be and passing away. You use names for things as though they rigidly, persistently endured; yet even the stream into which you step a second time is not the one you stepped into before.[8]

Nietzsche here echoes the Greek philosopher Heraclitus: nothing abides, everything flows; we cannot step into the same river twice. Still, most of us most of the time take the things of this world, particularly ourselves—to which we attach our beloved names—to be firm and fixed. We are led into this error by our "myopia." Our vision is weak and so we only apprehend what appears nearby and in the short term. More to the point, our myopia is intensified by the very language on which we depend to transact our daily business.

Consider the word "tree." We use it to label the tall thing growing in our backyard as well as the trees in the forest and the one on the street. All these particular items are in the realm of what Nietzsche calls "becoming." A while back they were merely seeds. Then they became saplings and grew to maturity. Eventually they will die. They are irrevocably implicated in a continuous process of coming-to-be and rotting-away. By contrast, or so it may seem, the word "tree" somehow refers to, but is distinct from, all of the particular items it names. We repeatedly use this same one word even as old trees die and new ones grow. It thus may be tempting to think that "tree" refers to something that, unlike the many individuals appearing on our screens, does not change. Perhaps, this line of thought runs, the word we use refers to some Essence or Form of tree that stays constant even as all the trees in the forest and the yard continuously change. Perhaps it is ontologically superior to, or even responsible for, the particular trees being what they are. This, for Nietzsche at least, is linguistically induced myopia at its worst.[9]

For all these reasons, then, ordinary language, bound to its subjects and predicates, and governed by the rules of syntax, is unable to give voice to "primordial pain in the heart of the primal unity." This task requires the flow of music.

Recall: William James made a similar point in his discussion of the mystical experience, the extraordinary moment of merger with the totality of the universe. One of its key features is its "ineffability": it cannot be described in words. By contrast, he says, music can give us "ontological messages which non-musical criticism is unable to contradict, although it may laugh at our foolishness." Such messages are readily challenged by "non-musical criticism"—by the sober, waking consciousness of an analytical mind demanding talk, and thus the rigid distinction of subject and predicate. In music such distinctions dissolve. For just this reason, it is the only medium in which the Dionysian, the counterpoint to Apollinian individuation, can possibly be, not only expressed, but also felt.

In their lyric poetry, Nietzsche argues, the Greeks, cognizant of the limitations of the Apollinian, strove to make language sing. How the verses of Archilochus, the poet he identifies as the founder of the genre, actually did this is irrelevant here. What matters is only the general point he wants to make: there was more to Greek art than the clean lines of sculpture and the distinct elements of Homeric simile. There was the Dionysian. Most important of all, there was tragedy.

The theatre was a central institution in Athenian civic culture, and Dionysus was its god. Each spring as many as sixteen thousand citizens would gather as a grand audience for the plays of Aeschylus, Sophocles, and Euripides (as well as those of Aristophanes, since comedies were also performed). The festivities began with a procession in which the crowds would escort a statue of Dionysus into the theatre, located near the Acropolis. Songs would be sung, giant phalloi would be carried along the route, wine would pour. The next day would feature another procession, this time of those children who had been orphaned in war. In honor of their fathers' sacrifice for the city, they would get front-row seats. Then came the show: tragedies and comedies. All were performed as entries in a competition. Those few plays that have managed to survive the 2,500 years of transmission were typically the winners.

The young Nietzsche was enthralled by the tragedies. Unlike lyric poetry, a genre which strained to imitate music, classical Athenian tragedy actually built music into itself. It was performed by two or three actors accompanied by a chorus of twelve or fifteen. All the men on stage—for there were no women— wore large masks. Just as we saw in our reading of the *Bacchae*, the play alternated between discrete episodes in which the actors spoke in the language of "Apollinian precision and lucidity" (p. 67) and choral interludes of song and dance. This "mysterious union" (p. 47) of music and language was, according to Nietzsche, tragedy's fusion of the Apollinian form-impulse and the organic solvent of the Dionysian.

Perhaps the easiest way for us today to imagine the effect of such a play is to think about those movies whose soundtrack plays a crucial role. The camera may bring faces into sharp focus, and thereby bring a powerful dose of individuation to the screen, but the music is the sustaining heartbeat of the film. The soundtrack, like the chorus of a tragedy, is a counterbalance to the movie's realism, a "decisive step by which war is declared openly and honorably against

… naturalism" (p. 58). After all, even in the age of earbuds and playlists, daily life is not really accompanied by music.

Nietzsche endorses the standard historical claim "that tragedy arose from the tragic chorus" (p. 56) and in its earliest stages was nothing but chorus. But for him, even this understates the fundamental role the Dionysian plays in tragedy.

> We must understand Greek tragedy as the Dionysian chorus which ever anew discharges itself in an Apollinian world of images. Thus the choral parts with which tragedy is interlaced are, as it were, the womb that gave birth to the whole of the so-called dialogue.
>
> p. 65

The Dionysian, affiliated with the female and the wet, is incarnated by the chorus, which is the "womb" from which the individuated characters emerge. On stage they speak clearly articulated words and, as the plot unfolds, their monumental suffering is meticulously described. We have already seen, for example, the detail in which Euripides depicts poor Pentheus being torn to pieces by his own mother. The audience must have been wracked by this scene, and were the play composed only of such extraordinary suffering it could well have left them in despair. But, says Nietzsche, tragedy provides a kind of comfort as well. It reminds the audience that there is more to life than their precious little, individuated, suffering selves. And this it does through the singing and dancing of the chorus.

> This is the most immediate effect of the Dionysian tragedy, that the state and society and quite generally, the gulfs between man and man give way to an overwhelming feeling of unity leading back to the very heart of nature. The metaphysical comfort—with which, I am suggesting even now, every true tragedy leaves us—that life is at the bottom of things, despite all the changes of appearances, indestructibly powerful and pleasurable—this comfort appears in the incarnate clarity in the chorus.
>
> p. 59

Perhaps Nietzsche's words are meant to recall the extraordinary scene in the *Bacchae* (694–711), where the shepherd describes the Maenads frolicking in the mountain woods. Snakes lick their cheeks; the earth flows with milk, honey, and wine; the women are one with flora and fauna. Yes, we will suffer and die. But we are alive and part of a vast and teeming ecosystem. When the audience is drawn into the song and dance of the chorus it can experience, however briefly, such a feeling of unity. Thus, says Nietzsche, does the chorus offer "metaphysical comfort." We are not solitary creatures who suffer alone, for we are more than ourselves.

It may now seem that Nietzsche is offering conflicting descriptions of the Dionysian. On the one hand, there is the lament of Achilles, for whom even the paltry life of a worthless slave would be superior to the nothingness of death. His speech, says Nietzsche, expresses the terror the Greeks felt at the prospect of annihilation, and it was the energizing goad leading them to create sculpture and epic poetry, those beautiful illusions which bathe us in the light of stable presence. In this view, the individuating force of the Apollinian saved them from the terrifying formlessness of the Dionysian. But Nietzsche also says that the Dionysian, expressed in the song and dance of the tragic chorus, is comforting. Which is it? Both. For in representing the "annihilation of the ordinary bounds and limits of existence" (p. 59), the Dionysian, like alcohol itself, is bipolar. It allows us to transcend, even if briefly, the daily grind relentlessly leading to old age and death. And yet the bounds and limits constituting our individuality, our little life stories, are what allow us to function on a daily basis—to stay, in other words, alive.

Are Nietzsche's flamboyant claims about the history of Greek culture and its arts the least bit accurate? This is a question for another sort of book entirely. But even if he was wrong about much, he was nonetheless onto something terribly important. Two competing forces are at work in our lives: form maintenance and dissolution. Biological activity, understood as a constant struggle against entropy, is squarely in the camp of the former. Organisms eat in order to keep themselves intact and separate from the surrounding environment. They (we) keep their shape for as long as they can, until their energy runs out. Human beings tell stories to do the same. But we drink in order to burst at the seams, to sing and dance and merge; to say yes to the teeming wholeness, the organic flow, from which we normally keep ourselves apart. It is a delicate balance, one rarely kept well. The young Nietzsche found the "mysterious union" of the Apollinian and the Dionysian in classical Greek tragedy, a hybrid of music and language, to have captured it perfectly. So too is it found at a really good dinner party, where friends, family, and strangers gather to share food and stories, give shape to their lives, and drink enough wine to take off the edge.

In short, the good supper, the crowded table, is a tragic affair. On the one hand, it is a pitifully brief holding action against the transience of which we are too painfully aware. On the other, it may well be the best this world has to offer us. Next to nothing, but not nothing.

Interlude[2]

(12)

I've given several fabulous, blowout parties in my life. One was for my friend Steve in 1993. His first novel had just come out and had been well reviewed. We drank vast quantities, took turns reading from Steve's book (which I thought was excellent), and roared like fools until 4 a.m. Then there was New Year's Eve, 2008. Its theme was furnished by a Bob Dylan line: "It's not dark yet, but it's getting there." The economy, after all, had just crashed and the future, especially for our children, felt bleak. Danced madly in my living room with fellow semi-geezers. Had a huge amount of fun.

I took LSD and mescaline several times during my first two years of college, and these experiences, I think, changed me for the better. I learned that, just as William James says, there's more to life, and thus to the universe, than normal waking consciousness. The drugs, which I have not taken since, pried me open, and I'm grateful to them (as James probably was to nitrous oxide, the psychedelic drug of his time).[1] For this reason, I count myself a Dionysian—someone who, even if he doesn't drink as much as he should, affirms the goodness of, and the occasional need for, intoxication. Without it we are too little, too late.

Another bond with James: his empathy for people gripped by religious fervor, even if he himself, sober psychologist and philosopher, was not one of them. I too have long had an interest in religion and its people, even if I am in no way devout. In my first years in college, following the lead of those countercultural students who were seeking an alternative to the Western rationalism they held responsible for the war in Vietnam, I took courses on the Bible and on Chinese thought. They inspired me, opened me up to the fact—and it is a fact—that there was more to life than the math major I had begun in my freshman year. I wrote a couple of papers, one on Genesis and another on Taoism, while tripping on LSD. However juvenile they may have been, those experiences were joyful and decisive. Eventually, though, I came to understand that sobriety, rigor, steadiness, and clarity—my default states—were, for better or worse, far more in line with my character. I became a professional explainer.

Still, I acknowledge Dionysus, the bipolar god who breaks bonds and shatters the everyday, who says yes to it all even as he threatens us with annihilation. He emblematizes the religious experience itself. James insists that such experience is an indispensable feature of human life, and he is right. But he does so from the distance of the rational observer, the scientifically minded psychologist. Sometimes this seems to make him feel sad, as if he knew he was missing out. I don't feel that, although sometimes I do wish I could go mad a little more often. I get intoxicated only rarely. Maybe I should do so more often. And then write down the results. Maybe then my books would come to better life.

(13)

Because the animal ate only grass when it was alive, I cooked the steaks, which came from Chestnut Farm, on a very hot grill for only a couple of minutes on each side. Then I let them stand for five more. The meat was fine for me, Gina, and Charles, but too rare for Amy, so I threw her piece back on the grill for a short time. Dinner was just the steaks and a large salad, composed mostly of a mesclun mix from Atlas Farms. It's still cool enough for the greens to be sharp and crisp. I also threw in a sprinkling of mustard greens, and some string beans marinated in olive oil and balsamic vinegar. And, of course, there was bread from Clear Flour. The two bottles of wine were a decent Spanish red. Desert was strawberries. Fortunately, we got back from Europe before their season ended. We will eat them every day until they disappear.

The evening was warm, our garden was lovely—there'd been plenty of rain when we were gone—and we spent hours on our deck in the backyard. We talked a lot, mostly about Berlin, from which Gina and I had just returned, and to which Amy and Charles will go in the fall. We went there after our annual stay in Pisa and liked it enormously. The weather was gorgeous, and the cafes were filled with people drinking beer. We had good Turkish and Vietnamese food. The only German meal was a mediocre Wiener schnitzel.

Four other friends are coming over in a couple of days, and I'm thinking I will just reprise the menu. The cooking will be easy, which for me is always a plus. In fact, the only slightly demanding part will be the shopping. I'll have to bike down to the Boston Public Market in order to buy the steaks—or maybe lamb chops—from Chestnut Farm, and then over to Copley Square where Atlas Farms has a stand. It'll take a while, but the weather is fine and the ride should be okay. My friends will bring the wine, so I'll only need to have a bottle of prosecco ready when they arrive. And some nice cheese from The Cellars at Jasper Hill. Probably their blue. I'll get some more strawberries at Copley. I'll marinate them in lemon juice and sugar for a couple of hours before serving.

I feel smaller when I'm not cooking for others. Of course, Gina and I cook on a daily basis for each other. But when friends come over, it becomes more deliberate, time-consuming, bigger, and better.

One of the friends who are coming lost his 28-year-old son to a heroin overdose in December. He's slowly reentering the world. It hasn't been easy for us to talk about it. When we do, even though the words feel heavy, they actually carry little weight. Better, I think, to invite him over just to eat and drink with us. Good food. Ample wine. Maybe a few laughs. Next to nothing, but not nothing.

(14)

Strawberries are gone, but blueberries have arrived. I buy quarts at the market, rinse them, throw them into a pot, add lemon juice and a bit of sugar, and then keep them over the fire for a few minutes. The berries will crack but remain largely intact, and juice will flow. We will have them almost every day for breakfast and dessert during the next few weeks. Peaches are also here, and they have been terrific. Salad greens aren't what they were earlier in the summer, but the string beans are okay.

(15)

Warm summer evening, dinner on the deck with Drew and Anne. We gave them the two best seats in the house, the ones facing the garden, whose shapely outlines are visible in the near dark. Gina took advantage of the heirloom tomatoes that are pouring into the market and made a delicious linguine. Four large tomatoes, chopped and drained, a chunk of brie, basil, olive oil, garlic, pepper. Let the mixture stand for a couple of hours, and then pour in the hot pasta. Mix thoroughly. That and some string beans and bread. Drew brought a Barolo and an Amarone. We stayed out there for hours.

Despite drinks on the front porch, and breakfast and dinner on the back deck, there's a downside to summer. We become acutely aware of our neighbors, especially the computer scientists next door. They're on the spectrum, blind to almost everything other than their screens. Their unpainted house looks awful, the driveway is a shambles, the yard littered with play equipment their children stopped using years ago. Their two dogs, often neglected, bark hysterically. Across the street another family is as equally oblivious to our existence. Cold as ice, the two parents, probably tech, come home late from work. Babysitters are the norm. Their children are loud and aggressive. Future CEOs in the making. Because I sit on the front porch so often, I'm all too familiar with their doings and sounds. So, even when the weather is fine, I sometimes look forward to the cold and dark days of winter, when the windows are shut tight, and I can forget there's a neighborhood outside. How sad is that?

(16)

I tried making the pesto the way Alfredo does. While the water was coming to a boil, I picked the basil in our garden and then quickly threw it into the food processor with the slightly roasted pine nuts, olive oil, and a clove of garlic. I pureed thoroughly and then added the cheese—mostly parmigiano but also some pecorino Romano for the salt. The spaghetti was ready in a few minutes, and the pesto went straight on it. The flavor had some depth, but it wasn't as good as Alfredo's. (It never is.) Next time, more basil, and a dash of pepper?

3

Socrates

I The *Symposium*

Nietzsche's story describes more than the birth of tragedy in Athens. It also chronicles its demise and how its precarious marriage of competing yet complementary forces was eventually disrupted, and by one person: the philosopher Socrates. As the quintessential "non-mystic," he was the "true opponent of Dionysus."[1] His "audacious reasonableness," says Nietzsche, condemned intoxication to the junkheap of the irrational. Inspired by the dicta "to be beautiful everything must be intelligible" (p. 84) and "to be good everything must be conscious" (p. 86), he drove "music out of tragedy with the scourge of his syllogisms" (p. 92). His hyperrationality, his "one great Cyclops eye" (p. 89), dismissed the song and dance of the tragic chorus as no more than drunken foolishness. And so he extinguished the fire of the Dionysian and shattered the heart of tragedy.

The key point to keep in mind throughout this chapter: the "mysterious union" of the Apollinian and the Dionysian which Nietzsche found in classical Greek tragedy is also present at the really good dinner party, which in its own way is a tragic affair. If Socrates murdered tragedy, then he obliterated the joy of food and wine as well.

To introduce Socrates, we turn first to the *Symposium*.[2] It depicts a drinking party held in honor of the poet Agathon. Since the participants, with the exception of Socrates, are still feeling the pounding effects of the previous night's festivities, they agree to modify the usual format of such a gathering. Instead of drinking, they will only talk. (No small point, as we shall see.) And their topic will be Eros, or "love."

When it is Socrates' turn to speak, he begins (characteristically) not by giving a monologue, as did his predecessors, but by questioning Agathon. From this interrogation he elicits five characteristics of Eros. (1) It is always "love of something" (199d). No one just loves. Instead, they love him or her, this or that. (2) Eros "desires" (200a), and wants to possess, what it loves. No surprise, then, that the original meaning of the Greek word *eros* is sexual passion. (3) "It has a need" (200b) for what it loves. If someone already has what he loves, he would neither need nor want it. If my stomach is empty, and I am hungry, then it is food I desire. Not the case when I am full.

Socrates should have elaborated this third point. If you have never heard of white truffles, you cannot possibly want them. But if you have tasted them once, and do not have them now, you crave more. To love, then, is not only to lack, but to be aware of the lack such that you are impelled to overcome it. The more acutely you feel something missing, the more you want it.

The fourth characteristic is this: (4) Eros is essentially temporal. It wants its object "to be present in time to come" (200d). Those who get what they want, who have what they love, want more: namely, to keep it for a while. For human beings understand deep in their bones that what they have is slipping away. So they fight to hold on to it, to extend its possession for as long as possible. Socrates' example is health. Even if you are healthy now, you still want, and will strive, to stay that way. Eros, and thus human life itself, is oriented to the future. The more acutely you are aware of the passage of time, the harder you struggle to overcome it.

Explaining Socrates' fifth point will require a slight linguistic footnote. (5) Love, he says, is of the "beautiful" (201a). The Greek word here is *kalon*, and while it can indeed be translated as "beautiful," its meaning is broader. *Kalon* often means "fine" or simply "good." Socrates signals this by later describing Eros as of "good and beautiful things" (201c). His idea is this: human beings are intentional animals. We do not do or want things at random. Instead, we do what we take to be good to do. We want what we take to be *kalon*. If we believe something is bad or ugly, we avoid it. Of course, we are often wrong in making these judgments. Someone may, for example, think robbing banks is a fine idea. Nonetheless, even this person is striving, however poorly, for what he takes to be *kalon*.

After establishing these five characteristics of Eros (of human longing), Socrates dispenses with Agathon and recounts for his fellow symposiasts an encounter he (claims to have) had with a woman named Diotima, a priestess who taught him everything he knows about erotic matters. She explained to him that in desiring to possess good and beautiful things, the lover wants to be "happy" (205a), which can be defined simply as the condition people are in when they have the things they want and take to be good. Most important, she proposed a fateful revision of the fourth characteristic of Eros. Not only do people who love, which is to say all of us, want to keep the good things they love into the future, they actually "want good things to be theirs *always*" (205a; emphasis mine). In our desire for happiness, human beings, aware of the transience of all things, want to hold on. Above all else, then, we desire permanence.

This idea may be startling, but it follows directly from the third characteristic Socrates attributed to Eros: it is impelled by a negative. We desire and love what we know we do not have. And what we have least is stability or solid presence. We are, and know we are, incapable of halting the passage of time, which disappears everything into the past. Most of all, then, we long for what will not pass away. Therefore, Socrates reasons, in the final analysis human beings "desire immortality" (207a).

This is strange. In pursuing their daily goals, most people would hardly describe themselves as striving for immortality. And yet, says Socrates, this is precisely what they are doing. Does it follow, then, that we are engaged in a fool's errand doomed to pathetic failure? We are, after all, mortal creatures who will surely die. Such was Menelaos' line. Recall his dictum, "no mortal man can vie with Zeus." Socrates, however, would disagree. By his lights, we are creatures restless at our core, aware of what we lack and so ever striving for more. Despite our mortality—in fact, precisely because of (our consciousness of) it—for immortality we should strive. Not, however, in the literal sense, for that would certainly be unattainable. Instead, it is metaphorical immortality that most reasonably becomes the goal of our pursuit. He explains.[3]

All human beings, women and men, are "pregnant" (206c). We long to give birth and "leave behind something new and other than, but like, ourselves" (208b). Obviously, these words describe sexual reproduction, and for nonhuman animals (and most human ones) this is the only way an individual organism can extend itself, or at least the information encoded in its DNA, beyond its own death. Some human beings, however, aspire for more. Artists and architects, for example, may hope that their works will survive after they themselves are gone. Soldiers and statesmen strive for "glorious renown" (208d). They long to be remembered for their great deeds and the lasting impact they had on their communities. Such is the desire for metaphorical immortality, and it reflects, Socrates thinks, a fundamental human impulse. We chafe at the flow of time, and in response long to give birth to something to outlive us. So, yes, we should indeed vie with Zeus, even though, or just because, we cannot actually become divine.

According to Socrates, the most complete expression of the erotic longing for immortality is found in philosophy, which in Greek means "the love of wisdom."

To explain this strange—and for Nietzsche, deeply perverse—idea, he tells a story, a kind of miniature *Bildungsroman*, of a young man who, fortunate to have found a good guide, is properly initiated into the mysteries of Eros.[4] It begins thus:

> The one who proceeds correctly in this matter must begin, when he is young, to go after beautiful bodies. And so, first, if the one guiding him is guiding correctly, he must love one beautiful body, and there give birth to beautiful speeches (*logoi*).
>
>   210a

The erotic journey is, not surprisingly, inaugurated by the love of "one beautiful body." As is typical throughout this passage, Socrates is not forthcoming with details. Does he refer to the simple longing an infant has for a mother, or to the sexually aroused lover's embrace of a beloved? Whatever the answer, this much is clear. This first step refers to the most familiar kind of human attraction: for another warm body.

Strikingly, though, this stage of erotic development does not stay put for long, and for one simple reason: the lover will "give birth to beautiful speeches." (The Greek word for "speeches" is *logoi*, the plural of *logos*, which means not only "speech" or "language" but also "reasoning" or "thought.") More plainly, he will talk to his beloved. Human beings are thoroughly linguistic creatures, and even our love lives are decisively shaped by what we say. So, for example, the lover may tell the beloved, "You're beautiful." This little sentence, however innocuous, begins to rev up the engine of change. For the word "beautiful" refers not only to the particular person to whom it is addressed but also to the woman standing over there, and the sun setting in the west, and the painting hanging on the museum wall. The meaning of words is universal. The beloved, however, is particular. Herein lies the rub.

"I love you," the lover says. He pauses, and then continues, "You're so beautiful." Then an alarm goes off. Wait, he thinks, this can't be right. You are not beautiful. You are you, the individual whom I love. But does this mean that in fact you are not beautiful? That can't be right either, because you are beautiful, and this is why I love you. Now the realization, terrible in its own way, dawns: the beauty you have, signified by the word "beautiful," is shared by all the many other beings out there described by this same one word. This universal beauty is somehow in you but is not you. And this is what I love. Not you.

Socrates puts all this in his own words:

> Then the lover must realize that the beauty belonging to any one body is akin to that belonging to any other body. So if he must pursue beauty in form, it would

be great foolishness not to suppose that the beauty in all bodies is the same. Realizing this, he must become a lover of all beautiful bodies, and slacken his intense love of one body by holding it in contempt and thinking it small.

210a–b

The lover realizes it is "beauty in form," the universal signified by the word "beautiful" and applied to many particulars, rather than the flesh and blood individual lying next to him, that he loves. Language turns us away from the sensible particulars we see and touch, eat and drink, and toward an immaterial, intelligible form, one we can only think. This turn is precisely what Nietzsche warned against earlier.

> It is the fault of your myopia, not of the nature of things, if you believe you see land somewhere in the ocean of coming-to-be and passing away. You use names for things as though they rigidly, persistently endured; yet even the stream into which you step a second time is not the one you stepped into before.[5]

Language seduces (some of) us into believing there is a universal and stable reality standing above the many sensible particulars. The latter come and go. The sunset was beautiful for a while, but now it is dark. The man is beautiful now, but soon he will be wrinkled and sour. By contrast, the form of beauty, beauty itself, universal and pure, stays the same. Compared to it, at least according to Socrates, an individual is puny. For Nietzsche, however, this turn away from the ebb and flow of sensible particulars and toward the stable intelligible, inspired by the very words we use, is not only myopic—a failure to see reality as it truly is—but also pernicious. It betrays the pulsating rhythms of life itself. Socrates disagrees on both counts. For him, language is a trustworthy guide to reality and its lessons should be heeded. The best of all possible lives is one spent in the search for those universals standing behind the words we use. This is why in the first stage of the erotic ascent the love of one body is so quickly left behind. Realizing the gap between the form suggested by the word "beautiful" and the particular beautiful body inspiring the *logos*, the young lover in Socrates' story dismisses the individual as something small and becomes "a lover of all beautiful bodies." This does not mean he becomes a perpetual seducer, always on the hunt. Instead, it means his attention is shifting. What arouses him is no longer a single person but the idea, the essence, of beauty—beauty itself, which all beautiful particulars share, and which is named by the one word used to describe them.

The lover's next move, then, is to "consider the beauty in soul (*psuchê*) to be superior to that in the body" (210b). What becomes increasingly attractive to the lover is the quality of the beloved's character, which is revealed by what he says and how he thinks, rather than how he looks. Conversation becomes more important than physical embrace.

Following this comes a turn to what Socrates calls the love of "practices and laws" (210c). Here he has in mind a person animated by love of country, someone we would today call a patriot. Socrates offers precious little explanation here, but the story might be this. The young lover, a restless soul, uncomfortable in his own skin, has begun the process of turning away from particulars. He has come to take what people say as far more important than how they look. Because he is now on the hunt for the universal, he turns next to his political community. He redirects his erotic energy toward its well-being, rather than just his own. He goes into politics with the hope of enhancing the community through the betterment of its "practices and laws." Once again, corresponding to this shift comes a diminution of the love he had previously felt for individuals. Compared to the political arena in which he now strives to make his mark, they feel small to him. In fact, as Socrates puts it, someone who takes the love of an individual seriously is like a "slave" (201d).

In the next chapter of the erotic ascent, the lover is "led to the various kinds of knowledge" (210d). Again, Socrates offers no explanation. Perhaps the story is this. Political activity is a competitive, often quite dirty, affair in which participants struggle to advance their own agendas. No one, except an idealized version of an absolute tyrant, gets everything he wants. This frustrates our emerging lover and he eventually realizes he will not find abiding satisfaction in the compromised arena of political action. He longs for something more comprehensive, better, cleaner. And so he turns to the "various kinds of knowledge." Perhaps he falls in love with geometry, whose proofs he finds captivating. Unlike a political debate, they are perfectly clear, objectively demonstrable, universally applicable, and thoroughly stable. In turning to them, our lover takes a significant step away from the human world.

Ultimately, however, even the "various kinds of knowledge"—the mathematical or natural sciences, for instance—disappoint him, for they too are limited by their particularity. Arithmetic studies numbers, not the stars. Geology studies the earth, not living organisms. Like every ordinary discipline, they are restricted to their specific, determinate fields. The lover, however, is on a quest for more. Stoked by dissatisfaction, restless head to toe, looking for complete satisfaction, he demands an erotic object, a kind of beauty, unlike any found in the political arena or in the sciences—one without blemish and, unlike numbers or stars, not constrained by particularity. Socrates explains what this might be:

For the lover who has been educated in erotic matters up to this point, having beheld beautiful things in proper sequential order, and having reached the final rung on the erotic ladder, will suddenly see something beautiful that is amazing in its nature. This is that for the sake of which all his previous labors have been.

First of all, it always is and neither comes to be nor perishes; neither does it grow nor does it diminish. It is not beautiful in one way, and ugly in another. Nor is it beautiful at one time, and ugly at another. It is not beautiful relative to one thing and ugly relative to another, nor is it beautiful here but ugly there by being beautiful to some but ugly to others. Its beauty is not found in the appearance of a face or hands or anything bodily at all. It is not some speech or knowledge. It is not in something else, like an animal or the earth or the sky or anything at all. Instead, it is itself with respect to itself, it is with itself, always being singular of form.

210e–211b

The Form of Beauty is the most lovable of all possible objects and thus the culmination of the erotic ascent. It is, in other words, what all human beings ultimately desire, whether they realize this or not. But what exactly is it? Perhaps disappointingly, Socrates' description of the Form is almost entirely negative. It does not come or go or change. It is not in the eyes of the beholder. It just is. Or, as he puts it, it is "itself with respect to itself." Utterly independent, impervious to the destructive power of time or the relativizing force of perspective, the Form of Beauty is utterly unlike all previous objects of the lover's desire. It is absolute, and it is responsible for the beauty present in all the particulars we see with our eyes or touch with our hands, and which we call "beautiful." The painting in the museum, the welcome smile, the meticulously crafted geometric proof, all gain their beauty by somehow participating in the Form of Beauty. Its universality is instantiated and manifested in those particulars. Socrates is silent on how this actually occurs.[6] He does describe, though, what it is like for the lover to finally reach this, the highest rung on the erotic ladder, and there to apprehend the Form itself.

If ever you see this, it won't seem to you to be comparable to gold or clothes or beautiful boys and youths. When you see such things now, you and many others are blown away. You feel eager, when you see your beloveds, always to be with them, if only you could, and neither to eat nor drink, but only to behold and be with them. So what would we think if someone could see Beauty Itself, flawless, pure, unmixed, free from human flesh and colors and all other such mortal nonsense; divine Beauty Itself, singular of form? Do you think it would be a paltry life for the human being who has such a vision?

211d–e

Even in its most mundane, its lowest, manifestation—the love of a single beautiful body—Eros packs a powerful punch. Madly in love with him or her, we care for nothing else, and so we lose interest in food and drink. Consider, then, what it would be like to behold not just a beautiful him or her but Beauty Itself. The experience would be transformative, and philosophy, the love of wisdom, the desire to understand and articulate the universal, is born. For only philosophy, Socrates says, affords us access to the truth, to what is really real. Without it, we would remain mired in the paltry flux of the particulars. We would live in the realm of "images" (212a). This word, which in Greek is *eidola*, is the same one Homer uses to describe the shadowy dead who dwell in Hades. Bereft of all substantive reality, they are nonentities whose existence, such as it parasitically is, depends entirely on the living. In the *Symposium*, Socrates uses *eidola* to describe the very things most people, and surely Homer, count as most real: flesh and blood particulars, which come into being and then pass away; red meat, which is grilled and then eaten.

Such is the radical upheaval Socrates engineers. By his lights, the world we see, hear, taste, and smell is no more than a fleeting image of a higher, more substantial and permanent reality, one apprehensible only by the intellect.[7]

Those who buy into this Socratic line of thought will have precious little interest in the dinner table, where food is piled high, glasses are full, and stories are shared. They will be too busy talking and trying to figure out what Beauty Itself really is.

II Socrates' Metaphorical Feast

The last scene of the *Symposium* is a wonder, and a few words must be said about it. Alcibiades, a beautiful, politically ambitious, highly intelligent young aristocrat, crashes the party. He is roaring drunk, wearing a garland on his head, and accompanied by a flute girl. He quickly convinces the men to join him in copious drink, and their nicely laid plan for an evening of sober conversation goes up in alcoholic fumes. When Alcibiades is informed that, like the other symposiasts, he must make a speech, he agrees, but on one condition: he gets to choose his topic. And it will not be Eros, but Socrates. For it turns out that he is obsessed with the philosopher.

Alcibiades' drunken speech is an integral part of the *Symposium*, a full interpretation of which would have to take it into account. Here, however, only one of his many comments about Socrates will be discussed. The philosopher, he says, does not like to drink and will only do so when social convention requires him to. Strikingly, however, regardless of how much he consumes, "nobody has ever seen Socrates drunk" (220a; see also 214a). Socrates' actions described in the *Symposium* confirm this. Near dawn, after everyone else has passed out, he casually saunters away as if he hadn't had a drop, and resumes his usual morning routine: engaging in philosophical dialogue.

Socrates, it may now seem, is immune to the power of Dionysus. Strangely, however, Alcibiades says otherwise. He likens him to Marsyas, the legendary satyr (215b) and companion of Dionysus, and describes Socrates as infected by his own kind of "madness and bacchic frenzy" (218b). How now? Is not the philosopher, as Nietzsche says, "the quintessential non-mystic in whom ... the logical nature is developed as excessively as instinctive wisdom is in the mystic"? Why, then, did Alcibiades sense bacchic frenzy in this apparently most sober of men?

Because Socrates is in fact intoxicated. Not, however, by wine, drugs, or god. Instead, he is intoxicated by philosophy itself. He is madly in love with the Truth. As he puts it in the *Phaedrus*, when he sees beautiful (particular) things here on earth, he is reminded of "true beauty" (249d), and he craves only that. And so, in one sense at least, he is like the women who worship Dionysus in Euripides' *Bacchae*. When they flee to the mountain, they do so in defiance of all conventional stricture. When Socrates philosophizes, his erotic drive takes him beyond the individuals and institutions most people typically love. Uninterested, it seems, in a beautiful body or painting, indifferent to clothes, money, fame, or political power, tempted not at all by food and drink, the philosopher's "Cyclops eye" is focused on a single prize: the universality of Beauty Itself. In his own way, then, he too has gone mad. Like a Dionysian, he transgresses the boundaries of ordinary life.

Socrates' madness, however, is of a supremely sober sort. For him, there is no song or dance, just reason and talk. Whatever bacchic frenzy he may experience, it is, at best, metaphorical.[8]

Earlier, the phrase "metaphorical immortality" was used to describe the goal of the erotic drive. Acutely aware of our own transience, we long to leave some trace of ourselves to future generations. Most people act on this urge through sexual reproduction. Some do so through the production of artworks that, they hope, will live on when they are gone, or through great acts on the battlefield or in governing, which will be celebrated by future citizens. Philosophers are similar. They strive to catch a glimpse of, to articulate and understand, the Form of Beauty, which absolutely is forever. They long to make contact with, and thereby share in, if only intellectually, the permanent structures of reality. Such is their version of metaphorical immortality, which by Socrates' lights is the most complete expression of human eros itself.

Aristotle offers a straightforward definition of a metaphor: "a transference of a term from one thing to another."[9] He offers an example: a poet may describe evening as "day's old age." Doing so, the poet transfers "old age," a phrase depicting the last stage of a person's life, to the twenty-four-hour day, where it is not typically found. Such a metaphor, Aristotle explains, can be broken down into an analogy: what evening is to the day, so old age is to a human life. The genius of the poetic mind is, he says, precisely "to see such similarities," ones most people fail to notice, and to express them in metaphors.

Alcibiades' description of the philosopher as in a bacchic frenzy is metaphorical, for Socrates, immune to the intoxicating power of the grape, is no ordinary Dionysian. But he is mad, since philosophy, at least as he practices it, requires him to jump out of his own skin, to leap beyond the ordinary constraints of temporal existence, away from the beautiful body or the lovely table laden with food and drink, and toward Beauty Itself, and to do so entirely through *logos*, the Greek word meaning both language and reasoning.

By Nietzsche's lights, Alcibiades' metaphorical appropriation of the Dionysian to describe Socrates is actually a destructive inversion of it. Alcohol is, as James puts it, "the great exciter of the *Yes* function in man," while philosophical rationality, *logos*, is the "dry criticism of the sober hour," which "diminishes, discriminates, and says no. In Nietzsche's words, "wherever Socratism turns its searching eyes it sees lack of insight and … infers the essential perversity and reprehensibility of what exists." From a Dionysian perspective, the transformation of intoxication into a metaphor, the transfer of "bacchic frenzy" away from full-bodied wine to air-thin Socratic rationality, is blasphemy and a catastrophic replacement of yes with no.

Like Alcibiades, Socrates relies on metaphoric transfer to describe himself. Most important, he likens his philosophical *logos* to eating. A nice example comes from the *Republic*. At the outset of this dialogue, he is induced to come to the home of Polemarchus by the promise of an entertaining evening. He is told that dinner will be served, after which there will be a visit to "an all-night festival" (328a). But no actual food or wine is ever brought to the table. Instead, the only meal the participants in this dialogue enjoy during their many hours together is composed of *logos*. This is not, however, cause for complaint, at least not for Socrates. In fact, he relishes an evening of just talk and refers to his conversation as a "feast" (352b). He delights, not in grilled meats piled high on silver platters, nor on wine served from golden cups, but on questions, conversation, arguments, reasoning. Just as eating is the integration of food into the body, so too can the soul (*psuchê*)—today we would say "the mind"— through its *logos*, digest and be nourished by its objects: the Forms.[10]

Another metaphor: Socrates compares himself to those eaters who "snatch and taste whatever happens to be placed in front of them before they have properly enjoyed what they just ate" (354b). Again, he is referring not to food, in which he has no interest, but to *logoi*, arguments, speeches. As a philosopher, he delights in "tasting every kind of learning." He is, however, "insatiable" (475c), and sometimes, Socrates admits, he eats too fast.

Another metaphor: "Only the philosopher," Socrates says, "can taste the sort of pleasure that comes with a vision of what really is" (582b). To explain this mysterious statement, he describes three possible conditions in which people find themselves. They are feeling either pleasure or pain, or are in some neutral condition between the two. Next, he describes a familiar phenomenon. When people are sick, they think "nothing is more pleasant than being healthy" (583d). The simple relief of returning to normal non-pain feels good to those who have been feeling pain. By contrast, those who have not recently been sick hardly notice being non-painfully healthy. Furthermore, after an intensely pleasurable experience, a return to the neutral condition may actually seem painful. From all this, Socrates concludes that, despite how it may sometimes feel, the middle state is not genuinely pleasurable. True pleasures, it turns out, neither emerge from nor are followed by pain. They are pure, and subsist on their own.

To explain further, Socrates constructs an elaborate image (the terms of which I will modify). Imagine an underground cavern that has three major sections:[11] a bottom, which is flat, cold, and dark; a top, which opens at the surface and is warmed by the bright sun; and a middle, namely the path ascending from bottom to top. Now, a person standing in the middle who is not yet at the top but can see rays of light emanating from it may well believe he is already at the top. But he is not. Such, Socrates declares, is the condition of most people when it comes to pleasure. They mistakenly associate it with satisfying "hunger and thirst" (585b) and other pleasures of the body. In reality, however, eating and drinking do no more than return us to the neutral state. When we are hungry we feel the pang of emptiness, and so we fill ourselves with food, and the pang goes away. But soon we become empty again and need replenishment, and this feels bad, and so we return to the table. The oscillation of our lives—empty then full, empty then full—is thus like the person commuting back and forth between the bottom (pain) and the middle (neutral) sections of the cavern.

For Socrates, those who most enjoy "food and drink and delicacies" (585b), and who find their best fun in dinner "parties and the like" (586a), have no inkling of what true pleasure really is. They are like "cattle" whose heads are bent to the ground as they graze stupidly on grass. They never "get a taste of the steady and pure pleasures" (586b) that comes with the apprehension of what truly is: the utterly stable, nonmaterial, intelligible Forms. This comes only with philosophical reasoning and is utterly different from all metabolic to and fro. For only *logos* affords human beings access to "what really is"—to being, to "what is always the same, immortal and true" (585c). *Logos* allows the philosopher to "taste" Forms such as Beauty Itself, those permanent pillars of reality that truly are, and the pleasure of doing so neither emerges from nor returns to pain. The philosopher is thus like the person who has traversed the entire path out of the underground cavern, has reached the top, and is rewarded by being bathed in warm, bright sunshine. No longer attracted by meat and wine, which can only fill an empty stomach, his soul is nourished by Being and Truth.[12]

III Recollection in Plato's *Phaedo*

Socrates was convicted by an Athenian jury of corrupting the youth and not believing in the city's gods. Given what we have seen of him in the *Symposium*, this should not come as a total surprise. After all, he encourages people to transfer their love and loyalty away from what is familiar—home and country, Zeus and Athena, earth and table—and toward the intelligible realm of the universal. As such, he threatens to undermine the bonds on which social and political life depend. Just as Pentheus feared Dionysus would corrupt the citizens of Thebes, so too did the Athenian authorities fear the philosopher.

In the dialogue titled *Phaedo*, he is in a jail cell awaiting his execution, a sentence he likely could have avoided by proposing, through a kind of plea bargaining, exile from Athens rather than death as his penalty. He did not, however, pursue such an obvious legal strategy. Equally strange, and unsettling to the friends sharing his last hours with him, he seems untroubled by his impending demise. In fact, he seems downright cheerful. He explains why.

Death, he says, is "the release of the *psuchê* from the body" (64c).[13] On its own, this statement does little more than reiterate the standard Greek (Homeric) conception of death, which is highly naturalistic. When a man dies, he breathes his last, and his *psuchê*—which is etymologically related to *psuchein*, "to breathe"—leaves his body. In this context, *psuchê* means something like "life force" or "cause of life" and refers to a physiological notion. As we shall see, Socrates will drastically alter this meaning of the word.

Philosophers, he says, are not afraid of death because, oddly enough, they are trying to release the *psuchê* "from its communion with the body as much as possible" (65a) even while still alive. For their primary task is reasoning, trying to understand and articulate Forms such as Beauty Itself, and this is impeded by the body. In general, our senses do no more than distract us. As Socrates says, "sight and hearing" provide us with no insight into the "truth" (65b). Our eyes and ears are capable only of apprehending particular sensible objects that happen to stand before us. They tell us nothing about universals and so divert our attention away from the Forms, which are accessible only to thought (*logos*). For this reason, the philosopher holds the body in contempt and strives to separate his *psuchê* as far as possible from it. Socratic philosophy, then, is a kind of "purification" (*katharsis*: 67c) through which the *psuchê*—which in this context now means "mind" or "intellect" or perhaps even "soul"—cleanses itself of bodily infection.

The next step is this: given this description of philosophy, it is, Socrates claims, isomorphic with death, which has been defined as the separation of the *psuchê* from the body. In fact, "those who correctly engage in philosophy are practicing death and dying" (64a). In trying to think the Forms, philosophers are trying to leave their bodies behind even when they are alive. It would thus be absurd for them to fear death. This is why, he explains to his worried companions, he is not troubled at the imminent prospect of his own demise.

Not all of this makes good sense. Even if concentrated, intense thinking is a kind of release of the *psuchê* from the distractions of the body, it may well be that when we die, we will no longer exist at all, and so, unable to do anything, we will certainly not be able to think. If this is the case, then a philosopher should be as dismayed as anyone else at the prospect of death, for it means the termination of the activity he holds most dear.

One friend keeping him company in his jail cell, a young man named Cebes, raises just this objection, and to it Socrates responds. The *psuchê*, he argues, not only separates from the body at death—a notion with which Homer would agree—but it continues to live on its own. In other words, it is immortal. (With this move, the word "soul" starts to seem appropriate as a translation of *psuchê*.) Socrates then devotes the remainder of the *Phaedo* to trying to convince his friends of just this proposition. The only argument of his that we will consider concerns what he calls "recollection."

It begins with an example (which I paraphrase). You might say about two sticks whose length you have just measured with a ruler, "They are equal." Upon reflection, however, you must acknowledge that this equality is actually imperfect. The two sticks may, for example, be equal in length, but also be unequal in weight or width. They may be equal now, but after a week or two their lengths may change slightly. The point is this: the equality of the two sticks—indeed, of any two physical items—is always coupled with, and thereby compromised by, inequality. The sticks are both equal (in length) and unequal (in width). Their equality is imperfect.

In a similar vein, you must also acknowledge that the equality attributed to the lengths of the two sticks is only approximate. Even if your ruler marks each of them at 6.0 inches, this is not an exact measurement. One stick may actually be 6.01 inches long, the other 6.02 inches. Determining such a minute variation is beyond the physical capacity of your measuring device. Indeed, for the two sticks to be perfectly equal—to be exactly 6 inches long—the zeroes following the decimal point would have to proceed to infinity. For this reason, no measurement of two sensible items, those we see or touch or taste, can possibly capture pure, invariable equality.

Recognizing that the equality of the two sticks is contaminated with inequality, or is merely approximate, implies that it falls short. But short of what? Of perfect equality. This is the decisive move. Awareness of imperfection requires the calling to mind, however implicitly, of a standard. To recognize that something is deficient requires some conception of that which is not deficient. To recognize the imperfect one must somehow think the perfect.

Consider this simple example. I know I am not a great athlete. After all, I have observed great athletes and, comparing myself to them, realize how short I fall. Were I to have no knowledge of what superior athletes are really like, I would be unable to recognize my own inadequacy. Or this: if you have eaten only inexpensive milk chocolate, then you could not possibly recognize how inferior it is to a highly refined dark chocolate. Only by having tasted both, the bad and the excellent, can you rank the latter above the former. This is the point Socrates is trying to make with his example of two sticks. To recognize that the equality attributed to them is imperfect requires knowledge of a standard compared to which they fall short. This he calls "the Equal Itself." (In the language of the *Symposium* it would be called "the Form of Equality."). Unlike the equality attributed to sticks or any other sensible items, it is perfectly equal and has no truck whatsoever with inequality. It just is, and always is, Equal. As such, it is not a physical thing, nor can it be sensed. Nonetheless, when we measure two sticks and call them "equal," to it we are, however implicitly, referring.

This move is decisive for Socrates. Wherever he looks, he sees deficiency. Everything in the sensible, or what most people call the "real," world falls short in one way or another. The two sticks are equal, but only imperfectly so. The rose outside is red, but it will soon wilt to brown. The people in the city behave in selfish and stupid ways. The government engages in acts of cruelty. The food is delicious but is getting cold. As Nietzsche puts it, "Wherever Socratism turns its searching eyes it sees lack of insight and the power of illusion; and from this lack it infers the essential perversity and reprehensibility of what exists" (p. 87).

Nietzsche is not wrong. Socrates does take the sensible world to be essentially characterized by its imperfection. But for him awareness of its deficiency is itself a positive, for it calls to mind what is perfect, and it becomes the fuel powering human longing. Gripped by the negative, we are energized. Realizing I fall short of being a great athlete inspires me to work harder in the hope of getting a little better. Convinced my government is acting unjustly, I am moved to protest. Aware of my ignorance, I seek wisdom. Aware of transience, I seek permanence, ultimately found only in the presence of the Forms.

Back to the *Phaedo* and Socrates' argument on behalf of the immortality of the *psuchê*. Realizing that the equality of two sticks is infected with inequality and so is imperfect requires cognizance of a standard compared to which they fall short: the Equal Itself (or the Form of Equality). But where did this cognizance come from? Not through experience of sensible things, for these are imperfect. Therefore, Socrates reasons, knowledge of the Equal Itself must somehow be present before our encounter with the equality of two sticks or any other sensible items. Scholars call this sort of knowledge *a priori*, for it comes prior to, and makes possible, the experience of sensible things. Sense experience, however, begins at birth. Therefore, he continues, our knowledge of the Form of Equality must somehow have been present in us before we were born. When we become aware of the imperfect equality of two sticks, we are reminded of the Equal Itself, the norm measured against which sensible equality falls short. In sum, gaining knowledge of the Forms is not a matter of acquiring new information but recollecting what is already present within ourselves.

Next comes a leap. Recollection and the a priori knowledge of the Forms implies that before our bodies came into being the *psuchê* was already alive. Therefore, Socrates concludes, the *psuchê* must be immortal. Clearly, this move is problematic. There are, for example, other ways of conceiving a priori knowledge that do not require the soul to be immortal. And, of course, whether a priori knowledge itself actually exists is not obvious. Perhaps human beings develop the concept of Equality by generalizing their empirical observations, rather than by accessing a Form innately present within. Finally, even if this argument succeeds in showing that the *psuchê* must have existed before birth, it does not follow that it will continue to live after death.

Fortunately, we need not struggle with such arguments here. What matters is, as usual, a simpler and far more general point about Socrates. For him, the life of the body, its desires and perpetual interactions with sensible things—all of which are essentially characterized by transience and imperfection—is made possible by the Forms, purely intelligible beings accessible only to the mind. Compared to them, all particulars—he and she, Athens and Sparta, food and wine—pale in significance. Philosophical *logos*, in which the mind retreats into itself in order to separate itself from contamination by the body, is the best, and the most pleasurable, activity available to human beings. Only through it can be human beings be genuinely nourished—by the Forms.

For Nietzsche, Socratism is repellent. It transforms the meaning of *psuchê* from "life" to "mind" or "soul" and thereby wrenches human beings away from the world of flesh and blood, and steers them toward an abstract, lifeless beyond. With all its talk of purity, it itself is infected by

> nausea and disgust with life, merely concealed behind, masked by, dressed up as, faith in "another" or "better" life. Hatred of "the world," condemnations of the passions, fear of beauty and sensuality, a beyond invented the better to slander this life, at bottom a craving for the nothing, for the end, for respite.[14]

> p. 23

IV Christianity: Spiritual Nourishment

Nietzsche makes an extravagant claim in the *Birth of Tragedy*: "We cannot fail to see in Socrates the one turning point and vortex of so-called world history" (p. 96). He has more in mind than Socrates' influence on the development of Western philosophy and science, for he is also thinking of the most powerful force he unwittingly unleashed: Christianity, which in turn came to shape the entirety of modern European culture. For the Christian, even more so than the philosopher, turns away from the body and its senses, from earth and table, and toward the eternal—toward God. Christianity, as Nietzsche describes it, is finally no more than "Platonism for the people"[15]—a palatable version of Socratic other-worldliness that is easy to digest.

To illustrate this line of thought, consider the following passage from Saint Augustine's book *The City of God*:

> Then there is the beauty and utility of the natural creation, which the divine generosity has bestowed on man, for him to behold and to take into use. ... The manifold diversity of beauty in sky and earth and sea; the abundance of light, and its miraculous loveliness, in sun and moon and stars; the dark shades of woods, the colour and fragrance of flowers; the multitudinous varieties of birds, with their songs and their bright plumage. ...

> Think of the abundant supply of food everywhere to satisfy our hunger, the variety of flavours to suit our pampered taste, lavishly distributed by the riches of nature, not produced by the skill and labour of cooks! Think, too, of all the resources for the preservation of health, or for its restoration, the welcome alternation of day and night, the soothing coolness of breezes, all the material for clothing provided by plants and animals. Who could give a complete list of all these natural blessings?[16]

So far, it seems Augustine is not only praising the beautiful world God has generously created but also enjoining his readers to take pleasure in its sensuous delights: notably, "the abundant supply of food" nature has bestowed upon us. But then he, a Christian philosopher par excellence, abruptly pulls the rug out from under our feet.

> And these are all the consolations of mankind under condemnation, not the rewards of the blessed. What then will those rewards be, if the consolations are so many and so wonderful? ... What will God give to those whom he has predestined to life, if he has given all these to those predestined to death? ... What will be our condition? ... There we shall drink of God's Wisdom at its very source, with supreme felicity and without any difficulty. How wonderful will be that body which will be completely subdued to the spirit, will receive from the spirit all that it needs for its life, and will need no other nourishment! It will not be an animal.
>
> XXII.24

Just as Socrates transforms eating into a metaphor for thinking, so too does Augustine here transpose food and drink into the realm of the spirit. For him, the pleasures of the body are no more than "consolations" for those who are "predestined to death," which is to say, all of us. To count transient, sensible things—food, wine, birds, cool breezes—as really valuable, as Homer so vibrantly does, is a grievous error. For the Christian conceives of another Being, one vastly superior to anything we can see or touch or taste: an eternal God who, like the Forms, is absolutely perfect. Both the philosopher and the Christian, then, exhort us to transfer our love away from the particulars we find here on earth, and toward a nonmaterial Being, compared to which bodies and their delights are nothing. Only God can truly nourish our spirits and quench our thirst for wisdom. If you think your grilled meat and red wine is good, wait until you taste and drink the real thing in heaven.

There is, though, a decisive difference between Socrates and Augustine. The philosopher's love of the Forms is a one-way street. He loves them, but since they are static, impersonal beings with no feelings at all—far more like numbers than people—they cannot reciprocate. The Christians trump this with a better offer. Not only do they love God, but He loves them in return. And His love can be apprehended, not only by a few intellectuals, but by anyone with an open heart. As Jesus says, "Everyone who asks receives, and everyone who searches finds" (Mt. 7:8).

Still, at least as Nietzsche sees it, the similarity runs deep. In locating the true calling of humanity in a beyond, both Socrates and Augustine demean the particulars of this world. In their eyes, human life, transient and radically imperfect, must "continually and inevitably be in the wrong" (p. 23). Fueled by powerful longing, they seek fulfillment but cannot find it here. And so the philosopher, through thought, and the Christian, through prayer, look elsewhere, toward an unsullied beyond, which is eternal and without change.

Nietzsche, like Homer, embraces a totally different story, for he takes the very notion of a beyond to be pernicious. For him, the metabolic churnings of the body are the heartbeat of reality itself, and the Socratic unleashing of other-worldliness and the massive upscaling of this proposition by Christianity have been catastrophic. They have led to chronic fatigue—with food and drink, with life itself.

Augustine, no slouch as a thinker, would dispute this Nietzschean diagnosis. He would argue that longing for the eternal God emerges naturally from the human psyche, and so it is really quite sensible. He explains in his remarkable analysis of time—or rather, of "temporality," the human experience of time— found in Book XI of his book the *Confessions*.[17]

Temporality, he maintains, is constituted by a unidirectional flow from the future, through the present and into the past. Simple enough. Next, Augustine identifies another obvious, but no less basic, feature of both the past and the future. Neither of them is. The future will be but is not yet, and the past was but is no longer. Only the present is. But what exactly is the present?

> If we conceive of some point of time which cannot be divided into even the minutest parts or moments, that is the only point that can be called present; and that point flees at such lightning speed from being future to being past, that it has no extension or duration at all. For if it were extended, it would be divisible into the past and future: the present has no length.
>
> p. 221

The present, the moment or the now, is the only one of the three time frames which is. But there is, to put it mildly, a problem. It has no length, no duration. If, for example, the present were to be identified as a minute, then it could be divided into seconds, which would then be broken down into a past, a present, and a future. The present cannot, therefore, be sixty seconds. Nor can it be one second, since that too can be subdivided. The present, then, must be like a geometric point: incapable of being divided. But if it is utterly indivisible, then it has no length, no magnitude at all. It is no more than a gateway through which the future (which is not) flies into the past (which is not) at lightning speed. Augustine formulates the problem thus: "If the present is only in time, because it flows away into the past, how can we say that it *is*? For it is only because it will cease to be" (p. 219). Since all things in this world are in time, all things are essentially characterized by their own nullification. Such is the grim tale of temporality.

Fortunately, however, Augustine's analysis does not end here. Even though the present has no duration, and so is unavailable to us within the flow of time (within life on earth), it is available elsewhere. For there is God, and God is eternally present. But what does this mean? To be eternal is not to have the sort of infinite duration attributed to a Greek god like Zeus. He is immortal, which means he was born, grew to maturity, and then continued to live on forever. The eternal is essentially different, for it has no truck whatsoever with the past or the future. It always and only is. In Augustine's words, "in eternity nothing passes but all is present" (p. 217).

Everything in this world is temporal, and so comes and goes. Only God is eternal, and thus only in Him can we, who are "predestined to death," find refuge from the relentless flow of time.

In effect, Augustine is here constructing an argument on behalf of prayer. It is not based on any sort of biblical injunction. Instead, it emerges directly from his analysis of temporality. Human beings are acutely aware of the passage of time, unable to do anything to make it stop. For this reason, we crave the present, the only one of the three time frames that truly is. But the present is necessarily absent from human life. For insofar as it is a moment in the temporal flow, it has no length. It immediately becomes the past (which is not). Nonetheless—or rather, precisely for this reason—the present is what human beings crave the most. As Augustine puts it, "the present cries aloud" (p. 221). It beckons us, calling out that only it offers the hope of genuine, positive reality. And yet it is utterly inaccessible within temporal experience. He expresses this, the essential human dilemma, thus:

> What is that light which shines upon me but not continuously, and strikes upon my heart with no wounding? I draw back in terror: I am on fire with longing: terror in so far as I am different from it, longing the degree of my likeness to it.

p. 216

Human beings are "on fire." We long for what we lack: presence. We seek what cannot be taken away: the eternal. On the one hand, this is terrifying. Because we are temporal creatures, the present, which we crave, immediately becomes the past and the eternal is essentially foreign to us. We live in time and cannot jump out of our own skins. On the other hand, there is some measure of "likeness" between us and the eternal. Even without giving a thought to God or reading a word of the Bible, human beings have an affinity for the present. We taste it even in our daily lives. Consider the following examples (none of which is proposed by Augustine himself).

The chess player, competing against a worthy opponent, enters into a game governed by strict rules and limited to the small board in front of her. During the game, especially if it is a challenging one, she does not worry about tomorrow's appointments or lament yesterday's failures. She is exclusively focused on her play. The pieces are all she sees, all she cares about. Her world has shrunk to a square of eight by eight and, if the game is a good one, within it she is fully immersed.

Or think of climbing a steep and dangerous mountain. Each step requires great effort, and so climbers must concentrate intensely on what their hands and feet are doing. Nothing else matters. They are, it seems, in the present, not the future or past.

Or think of soldiers fighting on a battlefield. Bullets fly, danger is palpable, and their entire being is focused on keeping themselves alive now. Nothing else goes through their minds.

Or think of the intensity of sexual embrace. Yes, of course it is pleasurable. More so, perhaps, it is all-consuming.

Or think of the many varieties of "mindfulness" currently being peddled online. They claim to teach us how to pay attention to what is simply present—breathing, for example—with the goal of alleviating stress and improving the power of concentration.

And then, crucially for this book, there is the Dionysian experience of getting roaring drunk. Intoxicated, we no longer worry about how we will appear to others, how we will be judged, or what we promised to do tomorrow. And so we blab without inhibition, dance without fear.

These sorts of activities are powerfully attractive precisely because in their grip we feel thoroughly engaged and alive, thoroughly present. Ordinary life, inevitably fractured into the past, with its regrets, and the future, with its demands, feels paltry and diffuse in comparison. Fully immersed in a game, an embrace, a party, we escape, however briefly, from the quotidian flow—from what some, but neither Socrates nor Augustine, would call the real world. We seem to be here now, and this feels marvelous.

Augustine, I suspect, would agree that these sorts of examples support his thesis. Time, speeding from the future into the past, tends toward not-being. Only the present offers a foothold in what otherwise would be an inexorable and lightning-quick flow. Only the present is, and thus for it human beings, painfully cognizant of the passage of time, long. But because the present is indivisible and has no duration, it is inaccessible. Thus, the activities cited above, however powerful the grip we feel during them, are really fakes. During the heat of a competitive game, the climb of a mountain, the Dionysian roar, it may feel as if we are in the moment. In truth, however, we are not. The present has no duration, and so in it we can never be. Regardless of how alluring such activities may be, they are no more than sops or, as Augustine puts it, "consolations" for us who are condemned.

Ultimately, however, this human longing for presence is extremely informative and need not be futile. Although it cannot be satisfied here on earth, it can find fulfillment through a loving and hopeful relationship with an eternal Being, one with no truck whatsoever with past or future. It can be found only in God.

The upshot: for Augustine, the Christian philosopher, we have every good reason to pray to God, to look toward and orient ourselves to the eternal. Augustine thus ends Book XI with these words:

> But now my years are wasted in sighs, and Thou, O Lord, my eternal Father, are
> my only solace: but I am divided up in time, whose order I do not know, and my

thoughts and the deepest places of my soul are torn with every kind of tumult until the day when I shall be purified and melted in the fire of Thy love and wholly joined to Thee.

p. 230

Augustine is painfully aware that he is "divided up in time." He longs to leave the tumult of this life behind, and so he prays to God, whose eternal love is his only solace.

V   Homer's Nightmare: Soylent

This chapter has addressed two fundamentally different types of thinkers. First, there are those who, like Augustine and Socrates, cannot abide the passage of time. They long to jump out of their own skins and to make contact, either through thought or prayer, with what does not pass away. And then there are those who, like Nietzsche and Homer, affirm the tumult of becoming. For them, Odysseus' refusal of Kalypso's invitation to join her in immortality is paradigmatic.

The great indicator of how these thinkers stand is where they situate food and drink in their constellation of values. Homer has nothing but appreciation for the real deal: grilled meats piled high on silvers platters, and cups brimming with dark red wine. For Socrates and Augustine, eating and drinking are only at their best when they are appropriated for metaphorical usage. Our spirits, not our bodies, need nourishment. Our thirst can finally be quenched only by wisdom. For them, the actual dinner table, however necessary it may be to keep us alive here on earth, is no more than a burden.

We turn next to another version of this antipathy to food and drink. Consider the following:

Soylent.Com: When Every Second Counts. Soylent™: Food Simplified

If you've ever skipped breakfast after rolling out of bed too late…if you've ever missed a lunch because of a busy schedule…if you've ever had a guilty conscience over a midnight microwave burrito…Soylent is made for you.

Protein, carbohydrates, lipids, and micronutrients: each Soylent product contains a complete blend of everything the body needs to thrive. It turns a full meal into a one-step process. It makes things a lot less complicated. And when you're busy, it takes eating off your plate.

Such are the claims appearing on the website of a brand-new food product.[18] Soylent, which comes in a bottle, and no doubt is typically accompanied by highly caffeinated beverages, not only can keep a body churning all day long but can also liberate its consumer from the tedious business of cooking or washing the dishes. Industrious techies who imbibe it will be able to sit in front of their screens for hours at a stretch. From Homer's perspective, this is a nightmare of the highest order. On the other hand, however unimpressed they may be by the tasks the techies actually perform, Socrates and Augustine would at least sympathize with Soylent's promise to take eating off the plate. Like the techies, they too dismiss a good, long dinner party as a waste of time, and would prefer to spend their hours in philosophical or spiritual work.

In *The Protestant Ethic and the Spirit of Capitalism*, Max Weber analyzes this phenomenon of total dedication to work and its consequent denigration of food and drink.[19] He traces its origin back to John Calvin, the Protestant theologian, whose argument he reconstructs as follows. Because God is absolutely omniscient and omnipotent, he knows the ultimate destinies, both on earth and beyond, of all human beings. "Some men are predestinated unto everlasting life, and others foreordained to everlasting death" (p. 116), and nobody can influence or even know on which side of the divide they will ultimately fall.

The inability of human beings to shape their own spiritual destinies seems to render life hopeless and to be terribly unfair. Calvin (as paraphrased by Weber) responds,

God does not exist for people; rather, people exist to serve the will of God. Everything that takes place, including the fact that only a small part of humanity will be called to be saved (an idea Calvin never doubted), becomes meaningful only in light of their service to a single goal: the glorification of God's majesty. To apply the standards of earthly "justice" to His sovereign commands is nonsensical and an infringement upon His majesty. Free and obedient to no law, God and God alone can make His decrees comprehensible and known to us. He does so only insofar as He finds it good to do so.

p. 118

Weber finds a cold, hard logic in Calvin's reasoning. If God is absolutely omniscient, then it makes sense that He knows in advance whether a human soul will be saved or damned after death, and that nothing we do in this world can help us achieve salvation. "From eternity, and entirely according to God's inaccessible decisions, every person's destiny has been decided. Even the smallest detail in the universe is controlled" (p. 119).

However consistent Calvin's train of thought may be, its consequences are potentially devastating to the human spirit. Indeed, Weber describes the "feeling of unimaginable inner loneliness" (p. 119) that the idea of predestination generates in the hearts of its adherents. If our fate is both sealed and unknowable, why bother doing anything at all? In Weber's telling of the story, strict Calvinism had to be softened by subsequent generations of Protestant theologians. Human beings had to be given a meaningful task to accomplish in this life. Even if they could not know whether salvation was forthcoming, they could, and therefore should, act as if they were destined to be saved.

> It became a matter of duty pure and simple for believers to consider themselves among the elect few and to repel every doubt about their state of grace as nothing more than the temptations of the devil. ... Thus, the admonition of the apostle—for the believer to "make firm" his or her own calling—is interpreted as a duty to acquire, in the course of one's daily struggle, the subjective certainty of predestination and justification.
>
> A further type of advice was offered by those engaged in pastoral care to address the suffering caused by the uncertainty of one's salvation status. Work without rest in a vocational calling was recommended as the best possible means to acquire the self-confidence that one belonged among the elect. Work, and work alone, banishes religious doubt and gives certainty of one's status among the saved.
>
> p. 125

Calvinist thought seems to have taken a paradoxical turn. Inescapably ignorant of their ultimate destiny, true believers must nonetheless act as if they are among the few who will be saved, and to do so they must work constantly to testify to the glory of God and the insignificance of human achievement. Endless labor thus becomes the true calling of humanity, but not because it results in tangible benefits here on earth. Unlike the person who works hard in order to save some money to buy a house, and then feels the gratification for having succeeded, Calvinists take no pleasure in the fruits of their labor. Houses, money, and land have no intrinsic value for them. What matters is only the work itself. From this it follows that the worst of all sins is idleness.

> According to the will of God, which has been clearly revealed, only activity, not idleness and enjoyment, serves to increase his glory. Hence, of all the sins, the wasting of time constitutes the first and the most serious. The loss of time through sociability, "idle talk," *sumptuousness*, and even through more sleep than is necessary for good health ... is absolutely morally reprehensible. ... Because every hour not spent at work is an hour lost in service to God's greater glory. ... An unwillingness to work is a sign that one is not among the saved.
>
> p. 160 (emphasis mine)

Weber cites Benjamin Franklin's maxim, "time is money" (p. 77), as the motto of this "ascetic Protestantism." Calvinists work furiously, and may even accumulate great wealth as a result, but they do so only as testimony of God's glory and as evidence that they hope to be among the few who are saved. Because this world, when compared to the next, is of infinitesimally small value, they do not luxuriate in, or even enjoy, their riches. They just work.

Soylent's boast is that, because "every second counts," because time is code, it will eliminate the need to put plates on the table, or wash them when dinner is over. Techies can sit for ever more hours in front of their screens.

There is no need here to debate whether Weber was correct in his analysis of either Calvin's theology or capitalism. Even if he was not, he managed to describe a potent worldview. Compared to the eternal, nothing we can see with our eyes or touch with our hands amounts to a hill of beans. Meneláos' supper, on this view, is just a waste of time since "idle talk" and "sumptuousness"—the life blood of the dinner party—are mortal sins. Whether in the guise of a philosopher, a spiritual seeker such as Augustine, or a relentlessly hard-driving capitalist, such, Nietzsche thinks, is the legacy of Socrates.

Interlude[3]

(17)

When our daughters come home for a visit, our best times are over dinner. Although big breakfasts—challah French toast and blueberries, fried eggs and potatoes, bagels and lox—are pretty good too. One of my few parental triumphs, or so it seems, is that neither of our girls succumbed to the awful temptation—or should I say disease?—of anorexia. They have always loved to eat and drink, and they continue to do plenty of both. My younger daughter has become a fine cook. The older has a demanding job, and her love of hiking, camping, boating, running, biking, snow-shoeing, and partying keep her too busy to spend any serious time in the kitchen. But she likes going to restaurants and eating at home with us.

This summer they came without partners, so it was just the four of us for a few days. One night it was shrimp pasta and salad, the next it was barbequed chicken. After that came bánh mì, Vietnamese sandwiches made with pork loin, pickles, and mayonnaise. Another night was tried and true grilled salmon. The tomatoes are splendid now, and we had plenty of them. Cocktails on the front porch before dinner. One night at a restaurant we like, which has decent food and excellent beer.

It was wonderful making meals and sharing them, consuming large quantities of wine, and then cleaning up, with our girls. Some of this was accompanied by loud music, usually the Motown my wife loves. We work well together, and there are few things I enjoy more. Although after the first three days, I got a bit tired of the drinking and turned to water (mostly). No big deal.

(18)

I worry my younger daughter drinks too much. She has, God help her, followed in my footsteps. She's getting a PhD in philosophy. Also like me, she eats too much too fast, and drinks that way as well. Even as a toddler, she would guzzle stunning quantities of juice. She's a tall, strong woman, and so she holds her liquor well.

When she and her sister were children, Gina and I would usually have a glass of wine or beer with dinner. We'd also have people over for the occasional blowout party. Our girls must have understood that we both liked the buzz of intoxication. But they must have also realized that high times were never the norm for either of us. The vast majority of our days and nights were steadily uneventful, ruled by responsibility. But my daughter drinks and smokes far more than we ever have. She also takes a variety of medications, both over and under the counter. So, yes, I'm a little worried.

My daughter's life has been a struggle. She is extremely smart, and rather beautiful, but for whatever reason, she has always been an outsider. I don't know why. Although she liked several of her teachers, she hated the rest of high school with a passion. Teenage social life was a misery for her, and she spent many a Saturday night at home with us, watching TV. She fled high school as soon as she could, and never bothered to graduate. Instead, she found a college that would accept her without a diploma. Only then did she begin to come into her own. She was an excellent student, and her professors loved her. She discovered, without prompting from me, philosophy.

Although she is still gripped by fear whenever she has to speak in public, she has flourished in graduate school. She's also a marvelous cook and baker (even though she's gluten free). She loves to buy vintage (1950s, modern) furniture on Craig's List, and so her apartment is gorgeous. She has been in a nice, stable relationship with a woman for the past few years, and this makes me glad. And, since her partner was once a bartender, she's a wizard at making cocktails. Which she drinks at an alarming clip. Her dissertation is on Hegel. Fortunately she's smarter than me, and so I think she can handle him.

I worry my daughter drinks too much, and that I might be responsible.

(19)

It's raining and surprisingly cool for this time of year, and so I'm thinking that instead of steaks on the grill, maybe go with shrimp. It would be easy. We have two pounds, bought from Cindy, in the freezer. Maybe with fettucine? Start with oil, garlic, tomatoes, a bit of pepper, then finish with the shrimp. That and a bean salad, fresh bread from Clear Flour, and some good cheese from Jasper Hill. Too bad the peas are gone. Even if they invariably fall to the bottom of the bowl, they add a nice touch to shrimp-and-pasta. We have parsley and basil in our garden, and I'll use both.

It would be easy for me to hate myself, and throughout my life I often have. After all, what can be said for a guy who puts more into planning a menu than he does to actually enjoying the finished product, which he will no doubt just wolf down? What's to be said about a guy who prefers thinking to eating? Maybe not much. But, truth is, I don't hate myself. I don't think.

(20)

This time of year, even the sandwiches I make in the department's toaster oven taste great. Nothing more than fresh tomatoes and mozzarella. Pitiful, I know, to eat alone, hunched over the computer, reading the *New York Times* online. But that's what I do. In Pisa, lunch is in the piazza, either at Trattoria Rossini or Signor Mimo's, and it's with friends, and it takes a couple of hours. Still, what I had today was good. Tomatoes will be gone in a few weeks.

(21)

Slow Sunday breakfast on the back deck. Pancakes from a whole grain mix and spiked with wheat germ, corn meal, and almond flour. Best are the blueberries and peaches we heap on top. That plus maple syrup, Vermont's gift to the human race. Strong black coffee. Kenyan from Peet's brewed in a French press. Didn't forget to take my 81 mg aspirin.

As usual, the newspapers are spread on the table. More than a dozen people mowed down by a truck in Barcelona, on Las Ramblas, where Gina and I walked a few years ago. Happy throngs in a vibrant city. Lives brutally cut short. I have children.

Tonight we'll have smoked salmon and spaghetti with pesto. Once again I'll cut the leaves as the water boils and make it fresh. We'll finish this week's tomatoes.

(22)

Cod on Saturday, swordfish on Sunday. Two lovely dinners on Block Island, with friends who have a house there. The flakes of cod, cooked perfectly, were almost translucent. The swordfish had been marinated in ginger and garlic, and when it came hot off the grill, it was meaty, robust, truly a steak. A tiny spasm of guilt. The experts tell us to shift to smaller, more sustainable fish, like pollock and flounder. These we eat in the winter, when the grill is frozen over. Roasted with olives, garlic, apple cider vinegar, and parsley, they're not bad with potatoes.

Today it's off to the farmers' market. Extremely hot, so I'm thinking I'll just get some bluefish pâté, tomatoes, cukes, and bread. Maybe a few ears of corn, which is almost impossible to resist. I want to stay away from the grill, so if I do go with corn I'll just throw it into boiling water for a few minutes. Not my preferred method. I'll shop for tomorrow as well.

(23)

Tonight we'll go to a bar in the South End, where Amy and Ryan work. We got to know them when they both were at Lineage, a fine restaurant in Coolidge Corner, near our house. Food there was great, mostly fresh from the sea. It was just around the corner from our movie theater, so for years our typical Friday night was a movie and then a glass of wine and a bite, usually lobster tacos, at its bar. We went there so often that we became quite friendly with the young folks who were the staff.

The chef at Lineage was Jeremy Sewall. Amazingly, his place was located just a few blocks from Sewall Avenue in Brookline, which was named for one of Jeremy's ancestors: Samuel Sewall, a big landowner in this neighborhood in the seventeenth century. He was also one of the judges at the Salem Witch Trials, an act for which he later apologized. And he was a critic of slavery. Jeremy has quite a lineage, indeed. The lobsters at his restaurant came from his cousin Mark, who runs a boat in Maine.

Lineage closed more than a year ago. Jeremy's success there led to his becoming part of a corporate team that now runs a half dozen restaurants in and around Boston. They became so successful that he had to abandon Lineage, his first and smallest venture. The new places also feature fresh seafood, but the difference between them and Lineage is huge. The old place was modest and quiet, with only a couple of beers on tap. The new places cater to millennials who drink expensive cocktails. They are large and loud with blaring music and youthful voices emboldened by alcohol. The old place, in geezer-heavy Coolidge Corner, used to slow down considerably by around nine, just as we would typically arrive from the movie theater. We would sit at the emptying bar and spend many a leisurely hour talking and laughing with Amy and Ryan, and Matt and Brad and Rob. The new places serve excellent food and have a proficient waitstaff, but no soul.

Jeremy has four young kids, and so might be facing a million or more in college tuition bills, so I don't blame him for wanting to strike now while his iron is hot. But still, I miss Lineage terribly.

The contrast with Pisa couldn't be more stark. Some of the restaurants there have been in place for decades. Most are small-scale. I ask Alfredo how it is that these folks, usually families, stay in business. He says it is because they do not want to get rich. Living in a country where health care and education are largely funded by the government, they do not fear the future in the way Americans do. Theirs are steady, reasonably uneventful lives. Can't happen here. And it probably won't last much longer there either.

We said goodbye to Jeremy at the farewell party he threw on Lineage's last night. I told him nothing of my dismay. Instead, I just said that the place had had a good run, and we were grateful for that. Which was true.

Don't forget to buy mint for the cucumber salad! We could easily grow this ourselves, but for some reason we don't.

(24)

Yesterday's dinner was a bit rushed because Gina had to go to a seven o'clock meeting. Blanched a half dozen Roma tomatoes in boiling water, then chopped them. While the olive oil was heating, I diced the garlic and the few flakes of habanero. Threw them in for a minute, making sure the garlic didn't brown. Then threw in the tomatoes, added some salt, and turned up the heat. Splashes of white wine and a pat of butter. Let it go full throttle for a couple of minutes, then turned off the burner. Went outside and got the basil. Threw it in the mix. Got the pasta water boiling. Just before the linguine was done, turned the heat back on under the tomatoes. Poured the pasta, slightly undercooked, into the hot pan, blanketed it all with parmigiano. Mixed thoroughly with a few more freshly chopped tomatoes. Pasta, salad, bread, and a beer on the back deck. Quick and easy, the way I like it.

Unusually good sleep last night. Only got up twice, and only had a couple of crackers. So this morning I didn't feel the familiar need to take a cold shower to wash away the night's agonies. Got out of bed slowly, walked to the bathroom slowly, monitored pain levels. Stiff back, yes; knees aching, yes. But not too bad. Not yet. No pain when urinating, which is a real plus and likely the reason why I slept pretty well last night.

Off on my bike to the office. A gorgeous morning. Cool, dry, sunny. Unusual for August, when it can be stinking hot and humid. So why the rush?

(25)

We decided to eat at home, which is unusual because we typically go out on Friday nights. But these days, it's so nice at home. We're in that small Boston window, the salad days when you just can't go wrong eating from the farmers' market. Tomatoes solid, but only on the surface. Corn so crisp and sweet. My god. Cukes, fresh dill, string beans. Only a few blueberries left, but compensated mightily by the arrival of the apples. Still early on them, but they've got just the quality the industrials lack: edginess. Why go out when we can eat like this?

Gina went to an opening at a gallery in the South End. I stayed home. And I puttered. Decided on spaghetti carbonara. We had all the ingredients. Pecorino Romano, parmigiano, eggs, and, even if not pancetta, some nice bacon. String beans, cukes, corn, and tomatoes for a salad. Barilla thick spaghetti. Strong black pepper in the grinder. Parsley from the side of the house. A nice Valpolicella from Verona.

Had a tall glass of cheap white wine with ice, turned on some music, a surprisingly nice mix chosen by the great god algorithm, and then did the salad, which was easy. The beans were leftovers from yesterday, when I had sautéed them with tomatoes and garlic. Chopped two more fresh tomatoes. Scraped the kernels off two cobs of corn. Began the pasta by chopping the garlic and the bacon. Ground up a bunch of cheese. Heated the olive oil. Threw the garlic into the pan. Kept it there for about a minute, and then threw in the bacon. While it was sizzling, I scrambled two eggs. Then threw them into the cheese, mixed it all up. Sprinkled heavily with black pepper. Turned off the fire under the bacon, and waited for a text from Gina telling me she'd be home soon. Even though it was cool, I figured I'd sit on the front porch.

But then I decided to open the laptop and write. About how much I was enjoying myself being alone in my house, especially in the kitchen. Which I was. So why did I stop?

(26)

A dear friend was eating with us, so I went all out with a boneless rib eye from Chestnut Farm. The best steak I know. So tender and yet rich with flavor. Cooked each side for two minutes on a very hot grill, then let it sit for another five. The string beans were sautéed with a great many gorgeous tomatoes, then showered with parmigiano, and it almost tasted like pasta when it was done. The potatoes were oiled, salted, and roasted. The wine was a nice Chianti. The evening was warm enough to sit outside.

Eating lovely food in my lovely backyard, yet I was pummeled by a familiar sense of failure. My youthful ambition had been to write books that would save Western civilization from devouring itself. From the beginning, I knew this was silly. Still, my books have always been shaped by a hope not entirely distinct from that origin. This led to their being mostly ignored by the scholars (or such is the story I like to tell myself). I've never really blamed them for that. For in truth I was never a full member of the guild. And yet scholar, someone who writes books about other, much better books, is what I am. I've been stuck somewhere between the academic and the popular, and I didn't have enough talent to pull it off. Whatever exactly "it" might be.

We finished the dinner with vanilla gelato and fresh peaches.

(27)

Finally hit my stride with the pesto last night. Which is to say, I finally got the proportions right. Two large cups of basil leaves, half a cup of oil, a small clove of garlic, and a third of a cup of pine nuts, which I toasted slightly. Pureed thoroughly. Then added a mix of parmigiano and pecorino Romano cheeses, and pureed (pulsed) briefly. It went well with the linguine, and dinner was just that and an arugula-tomato-corn salad.

For tonight I'm thinking of a carbonara and whatever vegetables I pick up at the market later this afternoon. Also want to stock up on honeycrisp apples, which are excellent this year. Maybe a melon. And, of course, more tomatoes and corn. If there's dill, I'll get cukes and make a salad with yogurt and vinegar.

I'm a bit wary of my bike ride to the market later today. A bit of a schlep, since on Mondays I go to Central Square in Cambridge. But the real issue is my back, which I wrenched in the gym yesterday. Did no more than reach for a towel that had fallen to the floor. This is what it's come to. I didn't feel too bad during dinner, but it tightened up last night, and my ride to work this morning was a bit rough. I haven't yet taken ibuprofen, but I will if I'm hurting tonight. Right now I most look forward to a long soak in the hot tub later this afternoon. I'd been feeling pretty good recently, which typically means I will push a little harder in the gym, which typically means I will injure myself. This one feels minor, and I anticipate recovery. But I can't help but think about the next one.

Don't forget to buy potatoes at the market today!

(28)

Something a bit weird about eating strawberries in September. But that's what we did last night. Heaps of them piled on a Clear Flour pound cake. But the farmer from whom we bought them assured us this was a late strain, not an import from California. They tasted okay, but I don't like the idea. Something appealing about eating in season. Asparagus and peas in May, strawberries June, blueberries July, corn and tomatoes August, apples September. Fitting into their schedule rather than they into ours.

(29)

Only a few, rather uninviting blueberries for breakfast. Season is just about over but we weren't able to resist one more box on Sunday at the market in the South End. I didn't sleep much last night. Too much flying around. My seminar, which is a dress rehearsal for this book. And my Intro to Philosophy class, which features John Stuart Mill on education. And later today I will substitute for a colleague and teach Aristotle on anger. So I couldn't slow down last night, despite drinking some wine. Guess I didn't drink enough. As usual.

(30)

Super easy but entirely satisfying dinner last night. Bob's turkey salad (dark and white meat, mayonnaise, and celery), corn, tomatoes, cukes, a baguette, and a couple of (too hoppy) beers. For some reason, Bob only makes an appearance at our local market very late in the season.

(31)

The heirloom tomatoes are abundant, stacked beautifully on the tables, and they have now come down significantly in price. Some are still luscious, but others are on the verge of mealiness. Great for sauce, but not quite the crisp slice you want with your Bob's turkey salad and fresh corn. The writing is, you know, on the wall.

I may be able to get one more heap of basil for one more full-bodied pesto. Always good.

(32)

Both of our saddlebags were full when we returned from the Sunday market at Harvard Square. So much wonderful autumn stuff: honeycrisp apples, a half gallon of cider, peppers, potatoes, peaches, cauliflower, squash, late-season greens (mustard, arugula), cukes, tomatoes, fish, bread, cheese. The place was rich with colorful abundance. A rewarding time of year in New England.

Memorial Drive is closed to cars on Sundays, and so the ride to and from the market was especially nice. The weather was perfect. Cool air, bright sunshine, blue sky unblemished by clouds. It was on a morning just like this, sixteen years ago, when a plane took off from Boston and headed south toward the twin towers in New York City. For days afterwards, the sky remained crystal blue and, except for the occasional military jet, it was empty and silent. People walked around in a trance, not knowing what to think, at whom to lash out, waiting for the other shoe to drop.

The Roma tomatoes are terrific right now, and so plentiful that even the organic ones are not expensive. Last night, I used a dozen or so. Began by blanching in boiling water for a minute and a half. Then peeled and cored. Then chopped. Then threw them into the olive oil and garlic already sizzling in the pan. Sprinkled with salt and stirred. Brought it all to a fierce rumble by turning the heat way up. Added a clutch of basil. Stirred again. As it started to thicken, splashed with white wine. Then threw in a pat of butter. Kept the stir going. After fifteen minutes or so, it reached the right consistency. Not too thick, not too thin. Then threw in a large quantity of green beans, still dripping with the water that washed them. Stirred it all together. Turned the heat down, and covered the pan for a couple of minutes. Then opened. Stirred again. Turned the heat off and let it sit. Sprinkled with lots of parm. Really good.

Extraordinary, baffling, horrifying shooting in Las Vegas a few days ago. Dozens killed, hundreds wounded. No motive, apparently. Just a black hole.

(33)

My ride to the Wine Bottega was wet. I had foolishly relied on the screen, which assured me there was only a 10 percent chance of rain, and so I left my jacket home. Sure enough, it poured while I was on the esplanade. I took refuge under a bridge for a half hour and then, soaking, finally made it to the North End. There I met Francesco, who knows a vast amount about wine. He helped me choose a dozen bottles, which should last a while. It's getting dark and cool, and so we're in the mood for red.

After the wine, we went across the street to the Boston Public Market, where I introduced Francesco to Red's Seafood, long cases of beautiful fish, and Chestnut Farm, the best meat I know. It impressed him, even though he's more than familiar with gorgeous food. The highlight was the Shrub Lady. Dating back to colonial times, shrubs are blends of apple cider vinegar and fruit syrups, cut with herbs. Pineapple basil, raspberry bergamot, chili lime. We were given tastes of them all. Francesco was thinking cocktails, while I prefer them with just sparkling water. But the Shrub Lady suggested a recipe that I will try this week. Shredded carrots, which the farmers have in abundance, with an apple cinnamon shrub and avocado oil dressing. (Two to one, in favor of the oil.) I can imagine the apple livening the carrots nicely. They both belong to the fall. Plus, I've never tried avocado oil.

I made chicken wings last night. Bought from Copicut Farms, whose birds are raised outdoors and actually are free to forage. They're meatier and juicier than any I know. Marinated them in (cheap) balsamic vinegar, ketchup, a bit of tamari, hot sauce and honey, and olive oil. Moist and good. Worried a bit about undercooking. Industrialized chicken is horrifying. (Sixty billion, filled with antibiotics, slaughtered every year.) I'm hoping that the moistness of the wings signaled not undercooking but the way they were raised. Copicut claims their own slaughterhouse is super-sanitary. I don't usually eat meat when I don't know where it's from. These wings were delicious, and so I'm thinking about buying a few whole chickens for the winter.

A joke I heard in a Woody Allen movie: This guy goes to a psychiatrist. He tells him that his sister thinks she's a chicken. The doctor assures him that he can cure her. Oh no, don't do that, the guy says. We need the eggs.

(34)

Such a warm autumn, and the tomatoes are brimming at the markets. It's still possible to get an heirloom or two for slicing, but the real treat has been the abundance of San Marzano and other varieties for sauce. Our dinners recently have consisted mostly of just pasta and tomato sauce. Lots of olive oil, some garlic, basil, a pinch of salt, and then cook those suckers down on a high heat, adding white wine when the need arises. Throw the hot pasta in and shower it with parmigiano. That and a vegetable, even an industrial one, makes for a fine little meal.

Truck terrorist killed eight people on the Hudson River bike path, a place where Gina and I ride whenever we're in New York.

The tomatoes won't last, and I'll be sad when they're gone. That's when I start to shift to the oven: roasts, brisket, chicken, potatoes, white fish. Good stuff all, but not my first choice. For weeks, it's been just a toasted bagel with fresh mozzarella cheese for lunch. And a honeycrisp apple. Tart, firm, sweet, tasty. My favorite. I've been buying them in large numbers, and my fridge is still full. But they won't last either.

(35)

Dismal tomato, pale and thin. But at least we bought it from a farmer. There aren't many left, and they'll all be gone after tonight, when a hard frost is expected to settle into town, which means it will be even colder in western Massachusetts, where most of the farms are located. The apples aren't crisp any longer, but the cider is great. The potatoes, carrots, squash, pumpkins, turnips, beets, and brussels sprouts are plentiful, but it's hard to get psyched about them.

Next week, after Thanksgiving, all the outdoor markets will close, and during the long winter it will mainly be industrial food. It won't be terrible, but I will miss buying from farmers. It's far more time-consuming, and expensive, but I prefer it.

Gina made a lovely beef stew the other night. Used a whole bottle of cheap Spanish wine. More of that on the menu, I hope. I've been stockpiling chickens in the freezer. We also have plenty of ground pork and beef. Meatloaf coming. And brisket.

I have a friend who prefers winter cooking to summer. This means she's a better cook than me. In the winter you must patiently boil or roast for long stretches and carefully add your stock, wine, butter, herbs, and whatever veggies you can find. The result is complex and deep. Me, I prefer a clean piece of fish or beef on the grill, some pasta with fresh tomatoes and a salad. I like my cooking quick-and-can't-go-wrong.

4

Aristotle

I The Four Issues of This Book

For better or worse, this book has not really been about food and drink. Instead, its question has been, where should we locate them in our constellation of values? Is eating, with its repetitious cycle of full and empty, full and empty, just a necessary concession to our animality that must be endured only so that the serious business of life can be transacted? Socrates, Augustine, and Max Weber's Calvinists say yes (and so might gladly slug down a bottle of Soylent just to get it over with). For them intelligible or spiritual reality, changeless and eternal, infinitely exceeds the physical in both being and goodness, and the true calling of humanity is to turn away from this world and redirect our love toward the Forms or God. Such thinkers may occasionally speak well of eating and drinking, but only as metaphors to express the intimate contact human beings can hope to make with ultimate reality. Augustine again:

> We shall drink of God's Wisdom at its very source, with supreme felicity and without any difficulty. How wonderful will be that body which will be completely subdued to the spirit, will receive from the spirit all that it needs for its life, and will need no other nourishment! It will not be an animal.[1]

In radical contrast, Homer locates actual food and drink at the heart of a truly good life. Seated at the dinner table, well set, we know who we are: human animals. For this reason, prior to the meal an offering is made to the gods, a reminder we are not they. And then we pass around the platters, piled high with meats, and commence with the eating, drinking, and storytelling needed to keep us intact for just a little while longer. Perhaps it is Odysseus at sea, clinging "to a single beam" (V.385), all that remains of his ship after it has been wrecked in a storm, who best symbolizes such a worldview. By Homer's lights, we are all in the same, leaking boat. Over supper, at least, we find sustenance, for we are in it together, and the wine we are drinking, after it has loosened our tongues, may grant us sweet sleep. As a consequence, the cardinal imperative of Homeric morality is to invite others—family, friends, neighbors, strangers, beggars—to eat and drink with us, even if our provisions are meager. Failure to do so is a crime against our shared humanity.

Bereft of hope for anything beyond, offering no room for salvation, such a view is tragic. Nietzsche, in *The Birth of Tragedy*, tells a similar story. He argues that Athenian tragedy (especially the plays of Aeschylus) was a magnificent marriage of dialogue and music, of the form-maintaining Apollinian and the form-dissolving Dionysian. Both need to be embraced, and in their complementarity, in order to properly celebrate the human condition. Without the Apollinian (food), our individuality would disintegrate and we would die. Without the Dionysian (drink), we would be all alone in the world, with only our shabby little selves to keep us afloat. The table well set, the glasses poured full, and the sometimes raucous dinner party physicalize this "pessimism of strength" that can look human finitude and fragility straight in the eye and say yes. Of course, when it is over, the dishes have to be washed so that, if we are lucky, they can be used again.

To ask again: Where do we, where should we, locate food and drink in our scale of values? Are they, with Homer, at the top, or with Socrates and Augustine, at the bottom? As the previous chapters have tried to show, resolving this question requires taking a stand on four intimately related issues.

(1) Transience (also known as mortality, finitude, temporality). Like all living beings, we are oriented toward a future. But unlike the vast majority of them, we are acutely aware of being so. Consciousness of the passage of time, and the ferocious speed with which it flows from the future through the present and into the past, is essential to our being. What is in front of our eyes, we know for sure, will slip away soon, and there's a good chance neither we nor anyone else will remember it.

How we respond to the awareness of time's passage determines what we value and shapes who we become. For some, transience is an insult. Surely, they think, there must be more than just a quick succession of fleeting moments whose inescapable terminus is death. Surely there must be a Being, Socrates' Forms or the Christian's God, which is stable, enduring, perfect, which does not die. On such a reality these thinkers pin their hopes. Others, like Homer and Nietzsche, dismiss such notions as pernicious fantasies. Face up to the fact of your own demise, they urge us, and do not avert your gaze. Only then can life's gifts, especially food and drink, be honestly appreciated.

(2) Forms. As the cornerstones of intelligibility, forms make experience possible. Without them we could not distinguish between trees and dogs, stars and buildings. Life would be sheer chaos as we could not garner any information about the world through we which we must make our way. But the world we experience is not chaos, and traverse it we do, and so forms, stable indicators, must be present to us. The question, though, is, from where do they come? Do human beings fabricate them, or do they somehow give themselves to us? Is the world deep down a Protean flux (as Homer thinks), from which brief respite comes only through forceful human intervention and productive energy (and eating)? Or is it (as Socrates thinks) already shaped such that its structure needs only to be discovered? Is stability a useful fiction or abiding truth?

(3) *Logos*. We can understand what we say to each other only because the meaning of our words is general. When I say, "The painting is beautiful," I may have the one hanging in my living room in mind, but both "painting" and "beautiful" can also refer to any number of other things. This painting is beautiful, while that one is ugly, but they are both called "paintings." The sunset is "beautiful," just as is my painting. Particular objects and their properties, which come and go, are called by names, which seem to be (relatively) stable and to express a more comprehensive reality than individuals. Our language, then, hints at the presence of forms. Once again, however, the question is, what reality stands behind and secures the general meaning of our words? Is there a Form of Beauty, as Socrates believes, in which both the object in my living room and the sunset participate? Maybe not. Perhaps names are the product of the cultural and linguistic forces through which we construct meaning. Perhaps, just as food keeps us briefly intact, language keeps chaos briefly at bay by generating an appearance of stable universality, when in fact there is none. To think otherwise, at least for Nietzsche, is to suffer from "myopia," to be seduced and victimized by names. By contrast, for Socrates, language is a trustworthy guide for the philosopher on the erotic hunt for the grounds of intelligibility itself.

(4) *Psuchê*. This Greek word is regularly translated as "soul." Often, however, this is misleading. For Homer, *psuchê* is the animating force of a living being. When a man dies, his *psuchê*, the breath of life, vaporizes. This conception may seem contradicted by Book XI of the *Odyssey* where the

psuchai of the dead seem to have substantial reality. After all, Odysseus talks with them. This appearance, however, is deceptive. For the reality of these "shades" is ultimately parasitic. They must imbibe the blood of the living before they can speak, for in themselves the *psuchai* are no more than shadows or images, with no independent being of their own. As such, Homer's depiction of Hades is finally a symbolic representation of memory. The only life the dead have is found in the minds of those who are alive and tell stories about them (often over dinner). By contrast, Socrates in the *Phaedo* argues that the *psuchê* does indeed live on after the body has died, and its next life will be shaped by how this one was lived. For him, therefore, "soul" may do well as a translation.

Determining where food and drink stand in our constellations of values requires us to think through these four related issues. This book will conclude with an extended consideration of the last, *psuchê*, and Aristotle's conception of it, and how this Greek word should be translated in his works. If it manages to do its job, it will draw together the various threads this book has already spun.

II Aristotle as Zoologist

Aristotle's thinking takes its bearings from his enormous interest in, and admiration for, animals (*zôa*). He devoted countless hours to examining them, studying their parts, trying to understand how they nourished and reproduced themselves—how they, in other words, kept themselves alive. He invented the field of biology, with a particular emphasis on zoology, and remained a towering figure until Darwin revolutionized it in the nineteenth century.

To highlight the primacy of the zoological in Aristotle's thought, consider these lines from his treatise *The Physics* (his study of *ta phusica*, the "natural things"). "Some beings are natural (*phusei*)," he says, "while others are due to other causes. Animals and their parts are natural, as are plants" (192b8).[2] In turn, a natural being, at least as Aristotle understands it, is one that "has the origin of motion and rest in itself" (192b13). A bed neither makes nor moves itself. As an artifact, it comes into being only through the agency of a carpenter. It is, therefore, not natural. By contrast, the lion in the wild just is what it is, and does what it does, independently of any human design or desire. Thus, it is natural.

These ideas need elaboration, which will follow shortly. For now, the key point is only this: nature, as Aristotle conceives it, is most tellingly manifested not in particles or forces, as it would be for modern scientists, but in living beings. Biology informs his physics, his study of nature, and not, as in the modern conception, the other way around.

In fact, the centrality of animals in Aristotle's worldview goes even deeper. In *The Metaphysics*, the treatise in which he presents his ontology—his theory (*logos*) of being (*to on*)—he writes, "Substance is thought to belong most evidently to bodies; and so we say that animals and plants and their parts are substances" (1028b1). "Substance" translates the Greek *ousia*, which like *to on* is derived from *einai*, "to be," and it is the fundamental category of being. (Other categories, such as quality or quantity, depend upon it.) And its study, just as in *The Physics*, takes it bearings from animals, which are first on the list of illustrative examples. Aristotle is thus, one might say, a biocentrist. He can find no better example of a being, of something real, than one alive.

Surely, then, when it comes to the value of eating, the most fundamental of vital activities, it is reasonable to expect him to part ways with Socrates, who in the *Phaedo* denigrates the "so-called pleasures of food and drink" as being, at best, a necessary burden, at worst, a downright distraction. No zoologist worth her salt would agree.

We might now expect *psuchê* for Aristotle, the zoologist par excellence, to mean much the same as it did for Homer: something like "principle" or "cause" of life, rather than "soul." To reiterate, the latter connotes a substantial being capable of existing without the body, and so would be of no interest to the biologically minded scientist intent on studying *ta phusika*. At the same time, however, for twenty years Aristotle studied with Plato, who himself was decisively influenced by Socrates. This biographical fact might lead one to wonder whether the meaning of *psuchê* in his writings might, at least in some contexts, veer toward "soul." This book, then, will close with a question: Is Aristotle closer in spirit to Homer or Socrates?

III Form as Species

Aristotle absorbed one lesson especially well from his teacher: the primacy of form. This can be gleaned from a single sentence in *The Physics*. "Form," he writes, "has a better claim than matter to be called nature" (193b7). What he means is that a natural being is not simply its stuff. A squirrel is composed of calcium, carbon, and other elements, but so too are other animals. Only because it has a specific form (only because it is a member of a species) is it a squirrel rather than a duck. Aristotle takes all natural beings to follow this pattern. They are form-matter conglomerates, with the (ontological) priority falling on the form. This has come to be known as his doctrine of "hylomorphism." ("Matter" translates the Greek word *hulê*. *Morphê*, "shape," the root of "morphology" and "isomorphic," is synonymous here with *eidos*, "form.")

When it comes to a manufactured item like a bed, it is easy to distinguish matter from form. The latter is the plan in the carpenter's mind, or the blueprint she has drawn before she started working. (In a robotized factory, it is in the software of the computer.) Its matter is wood. In the case of an artifact, matter is more natural than form. A thinker named Antiphon suggested this by saying, "If one plants a bed and the moistened wood acquires the power of sending up a shoot, what will result is not a bed but wood" (193a15). Antiphon's little thought experiment can easily be extended to living beings. So, for example, when a squirrel dies, its form disappears—it ceases to be a squirrel—but its matter (carbon, oxygen, etc.) persists and will be recycled into another organic being, say, a tree. On this view—call it materialism—matter is more natural and real, because it is more persistent, than form. Just like the individual bed, the individual squirrel is an "accidental" (193a17) and temporary crustation, a shape that its material components have just happened to take for a brief while.

Aristotle rejects such materialism. He insists, to quote again, that "the form has a better claim than the matter to be called nature." Yes, of course matter is a necessary component of all physical beings, but in his hylomorphic ontology, form is primary.

To defend his position, Aristotle invokes two critical terms. "We call a thing something, when it is that thing in actuality, rather than just in potentiality" (193b8). The pile of wood in the carpenter's workshop is potentially a bed or a table; in actuality it is neither. Only after the carpenter has imposed form on the wood—only after she has made a bed—would we say there is an actual something in the room. Similarly, a bunch of carbon atoms may potentially be a squirrel, but they are also potentially a tree. Only when they have become integrated within a specific organism do they actually become elements of it. Most important, since every individual organism is a member of a species (an *eidos*), every one is in-formed. In short, form and actuality go hand in glove, as do matter and potentiality. For precisely this reason, form is more natural than matter.

Like Socrates, Aristotle here is taking his bearings from ordinary language (especially nouns). We call something a "bed" or a "squirrel" only when it is an actual, in-formed, hylomorphic being. By contrast, the pile of wood in the shop could become anything. It is indeterminate, for it is a potential bed, table, or chair. Of course, we might use the word "pile" to name it, but the wood in a carpenter's shop is there only to be made into future beds and tables. Similarly, we say "a squirrel," rather than recite a string of the molecules, when asked, what is the twitchy gray thing in the tree? In doing so, we signify a form. Form and names, names and actuality, are a team. The way we talk tells us much about the way things are.

One could quickly challenge Aristotle's reasoning here by asking why, in a book on physics, should the way we talk be the least bit relevant. In fact, his ontology could even be accused of being anthropomorphic. In prioritizing form-actuality above matter-potentiality, it presupposes the primacy of determinacy and intelligibility, features of form and language, both of which are constitutive of human experience. Radical materialists, both ancient and modern, would disagree. (As would Nietzsche and other Dionysians, who privilege formlessness over form, and music over language.)

Aristotle offers a second argument on behalf of the primacy of form. In his typically condensed style, he says only this: "A human being comes from a human being, but a bed does not come from a bed" (193b6–7). An animal reproduces itself, although not, of course, its individual self. Instead, it generates offspring of the same species as itself. In our lingo, information encoded in the parents' DNA is transmitted to the offspring. As the embryo grows into a mature adult according to its genetic "blueprint," it accumulates additional matter and eventually becomes a fully formed animal like its parent; it becomes itself. If it stays alive long enough, it will then reproduce and transmit its species-form to the next generation. In short, biological activity is thoroughly driven by the *eidos*. The vast majority of beings in the universe, however, are not alive. Nonetheless, Aristotle cites sexual reproduction as evidence of the primacy of form, not just in the biological realm, where it rather obviously belongs, but in nature as a whole. Is his science, then, infected with his biocentric prejudice?

Aristotle offers a third argument, quite similar to the second:

> Furthermore, nature, when it is spoken of as coming-to-be, is a development into nature … a thing growing, insofar as its grows, goes from something into something. In what way does it grow? Not from something but into something. Therefore, form is nature.
>
> 193b17–19

His language is cramped, but at least this point is, once again, made clear: in studying nature, he thinks first and foremost about living beings. They grow.[3]

And when they do, they come into themselves. An embryo develops into a fetus. A child is born and then develops into a mature member of its species. Organic growth is directed at an end (*telos*), which is given to the organism by its form. Hence, Aristotle again concludes, form is prior to matter in nature.

As a natural scientist, Aristotle was interested in everything. Stars, dolphins, clouds, earth, and air. He wrote treatises not only on physics and zoology but also on astronomy, meteorology, mathematics, geology, and psychology. All his many works, however, share a common feature: they are studies of forms. Even his work on strictly human topics—politics, literature, rhetoric, ethics—are investigations into forms, of cities, plays, persuasive speeches, good lives. So, for example, in the *Poetics*, he likens the "plot" (*muthos*) of a play, the organization of its episodes or scenes, to "its *psuchê*" (1450a37). In other words, a play is like an animal. It has many parts and, if it is any good, each of them contributes and fits well into the whole. For this it requires a unifying structure or form to render it coherent even as the episodes unfold on the stage.

To sum up so far: On the one hand, by prioritizing form over matter, Aristotle reveals his debt to Plato (and Socrates). On the other, with his hylomorphic ontology he breaks with his teacher. For him, all beings in the world (with the exception of the divine) are form-matter conglomerates. Forms, then, are not "separate," as Socrates says they are. Instead, they inform material beings. As usual for Aristotle, the best example is an animal. The twitchy gray thing in the tree, whose material components include carbon and oxygen, is a member of a "species" (which is the Latin translation of the Greek *eidos*). And a species is never separate from its individual members. There is no "Squirrel Itself," analogous to Socrates' "Equal Itself," which exists on its own, perfect and untarnished by material blemish. Instead, Aristotelian forms stand before our eyes, embodied, staring us in the face. The twitchy gray thing is both an individual and a universal (species). It is a squirrel.

IV Aristotle as Apollinian

For Aristotle, the entire natural world, from the earth to the stars, is in-formed and thus orderly, intelligible, amenable to *logos*. Indeed, his commitment to form runs so deep that it is tempting to describe him as an Apollinian. While Socrates preserved the Dionysian, at least on the metaphorical level where it describes his mad quest for philosophical Truth, Aristotle is, head to toe, the sober, industrious scientist determined to investigate all the many beings, differentiated by their forms, that make up the world. He has no inkling of or interest in what Nietzsche calls the "overwhelming feeling of unity leading back to the very heart of nature" that is generated by Dionysian intoxication.

To reformulate: because he rejects the Dionysian, even on a metaphorical level, Aristotle does not have a religious bone in his body. At least not in the sense adopted by William James.

> Were one asked to characterize the life of religion in the broadest and most general terms possible, one might say that it consists of the belief that there is an unseen order, and that our supreme good lies in harmoniously adjusting ourselves thereto.[4]

Regardless of what they see with their eyes, religious people experience the world as full and promising, not empty and worthy of despair. But they are not moved to such beliefs by rational argument.

> If we look on man's whole mental life as it exists, on the life of men that lies in them apart from their learning and science, and that they inwardly and privately follow, we have to confess that the part of it which rationalism can give an account is relatively superficial.
>
> p. 63

Recall that James identifies mystical consciousness, the fundamental antithesis of rationalism, as the "root and centre" of all religious experience. In its grip, what is other becomes absorbed into a comprehensive unity, and the individuated self melts away. As such, the mystical experience defies linguistic expression. It is "ineffable." Language, after all, is predicated upon distinctions. Different words (names) have different meanings and play specific roles in a meaningful sentence. No sentence, composed as it must be of multiple parts, can faithfully express the One.

Aristotle has no interest in the mystical, the ineffable, or in James's "unseen order."[5] His version of order, which is to say nature itself, is utterly visible, and his commitment to rational, scientific, empirical observation is unshakable. Consider this passage:

> All human beings by nature have an urge to understand. A sign of this is the affection we feel for our senses. For even apart from their usefulness, we like them simply for themselves. Above all others, this is especially true of the sense that comes through the eyes. For not only in order that we may act, but also when we are not about to do anything, we prefer seeing, so to say, over the other

senses. The reason for this is that this sense makes us know and clarifies many distinctions.[6]

Metaphysics, 980a20–26

Sense perception is, of course, essential to survival. Because I see the train approaching, I step aside to avoid it. There are, however, occasions when we enjoy a sensual experience, not because it benefits us, but simply because it is nice to do so. Hearing the wind rip through the canopy of a tree, I pause and take it in for no reason other than that it is pleasant. Just as Aristotle says, we do indeed feel affection for our senses.

His next assertion, however, is not as obvious. Is sight really the favorite sense of human animals? Surely someone—a Dionysian, say—might object and insist that, for example, listening to music is her highest and most indispensable pleasure. Still, Aristotle identifies vision as the decisive human sense, and he suggests why. It discloses differences. You enter a classroom and, almost instantly, see a variety of objects: other people, desks, tables, windows, books. You see them as such because they each have their distinctive looks. Now, of course one can distinguish objects by means of other senses, but not as quickly or efficiently. With sight we are marvelously well equipped to apprehend forms, and for Aristotle such apprehension is essential to the process of acquiring knowledge. (*Eidos*, you may recall, is derived from the verb "to see" and is most literally translated by the noun "look." Similarly, the Latin *species* means a "sight, view, appearance.") Indeed, in the passage above, he declares that vision, more than any other sense, "makes us know." To know, then, is to apprehend a form.

Aristotle's argument can now be broken down into the following steps: (1) human beings (occasionally) enjoy their senses simply for themselves. (2) We prefer sight to the other senses. (3) Sight discloses distinctions and thereby "makes us know." (4) Therefore, we by nature have an urge to know. Our sensory lives, much of which we share with other animals, give testimony to the innate human urge to gain knowledge. They are incipiently epistemic.

Each step needs to be carefully scrutinized, since Aristotle himself gives little by way of supporting evidence. Unfortunately, even if all his premises are granted, the conclusion may seem fanciful. For surely not every single person on the planet is actually busy studying or trying to learn about the world. This fact does not, however, invalidate his argument, for Aristotle only maintains that it is in our "nature"—that it is a feature of our species—to seek knowledge. This qualification allows for the possibility that many, perhaps even most, people will actually fall short of fully realizing their nature, for there are many obstacles that can stand in the way of any single person actually doing so (poverty, war, illness).

To sum up again: Aristotle is an Apollinian insofar as he takes his bearings from sight. Interested in everything, he spends his days making observations and studying the different forms, species, and looks that constitute the world. He would dispute James's contention that reason can account for only a "relatively superficial" part of human experience. Unlike his own teachers, Plato and Socrates, he indulges not at all in Dionysian frolic, not even on a metaphorical level.

This line of thought leads to another: Aristotle takes eating, which maintains an animal's form, to be the fundamental vital activity.

V The Nutritive *Psuchê*

Because he is the naturalist, the zoologist, par excellence, we might expect Aristotle to be aligned with Homer when it comes to his conception (and our translation) of *psuchê*. It is hard to imagine it meaning "soul" for him, while "cause of life" or "animating principle" sounds like it would fit. Sure enough, this expectation is met in the second chapter of his treatise *De Anima* (the Latin translation of the original Greek title, which is *Peri Psuchês*).

He begins by differentiating natural bodies or substances into two kinds: some are alive and some are not. Since all bodies have matter, what makes one alive must be something other than its body. In other words, matter is too widely shared among physical beings to count as a sufficient explanation of why one is alive and another is not. It is thus the form of organism that must be responsible for its being alive. Just as the form rather than the matter explains what differentiates a table from a chair, so too must it explain why one being is animate and another inanimate. And this is precisely what *psuchê* is for Aristotle: "the form of a natural body which potentially has life" (412a20).[7]

With these distinctions in place, Aristotle believes he has bridged what he takes to be the deplorable chasm between *psuchê* and *soma* that Socrates had opened in the *Phaedo*. By his lights, while the *psuchê* is not a body, nor merely a by-product of bodily activities, it is not separable from it. Instead, it is the form, the actuality of the living body as it maintains itself through time.

Aristotle illustrates with an analogy: "If the eye were an animal, vision would be its *psuchê*" (412b7). An eye is more than a material chunk composed of elements, for if it cannot see—if, for example, it were removed from the head—it would not actually be an eye, even if it still contained those same elements. For it would lack the form, the essential whatness, of an eye. Deploying this analogy, Aristotle reiterates, "The *psuchê* is not separate from the body" (413a5). Instead, it is like vision, the eye at work fulfilling its function, being an eye. In this context, "soul" fails as a translation.

Another analogy: To seal a letter, one might drip some melted wax on the flap, and then press a metal stamp into it. The result is a wax seal, a form-matter conglomerate, neither aspect of which can be separated from the other without destroying the whole. The *psuchê-soma* (psychosomatic) unity of a living being is similar. Thus, "there is no need to ask whether *psuchê* and body are one, just as there is no need to ask whether the wax and its imprint are one" (412ab6).

This second analogy, however, is quite limited. The metal stamp, on whose surface a shape is carved, is static, rigid, and external to all the many wax seals it produces. But this is not the case with the *psuchê* of a living being. An organism maintains its identity through time, even though (and just because) it is in continuous metabolic change. Its form, therefore, cannot be static like that of the metal stamp. Nor can an organism receive its form from outside of itself. Instead, it simply is the living body at work keeping itself alive.

This is hard to understand, but it will become clearer when Aristotle turns to the next section of *De Anima*. Here he discusses the most basic, and most illustrative, life activity of all: eating.

Every organism, from a mushroom to an elephant, nourishes itself. Every one thus has what he calls a "nutritive *psuchê*," which "belongs to all living beings, and is the first and most common power of *psuchê*" (415a23). Unless one is willing to say, without laughing, that a mushroom has a "soul," then one should not use this word to translate *psuchê* here. Instead, it means "principle" or "cause" of life. To be alive is to be ensouled or, using the more expressive Latinate, animate.

To tackle the question of just what the nutritive, the "primary" and "most natural" (415a25), aspect of *psuchê* is, Aristotle begins with a puzzle. Is like fed by like, or does nutritive activity take place between two opposites? On the one hand, an animal seems to be just what it eats. I can be nourished by an apple only because it contains many of the same vitamins and minerals already present in, and needed by, my body. On the other hand, an apple is a fruit and I am a mammal, and so we are essentially different. So which is it? Aristotle's answer is, both. Before I eat the apple, it is actually unlike me, although it is potentially like me. After I eat and then digest it, after it has been transformed and is no longer an apple, it has become actually like me. Indeed, it has become me.

It may now seem that a scientific analysis of nutritive activity need only break it down into two components: the food and the living body that incorporates it. What is most striking about Aristotle's own account, however, is his addition of a third component. As he puts it, there is not only "the thing fed" (the living body), and "the means by which it is fed" (the food), but there is also that which is actually responsible for the nourishing, for the unlike becoming like. The last item Aristotle calls "*psuchê* in the primary sense" (416b22). Understanding what this means is the key to deciphering his account of *psuchê* in general.

The first task of a biologist is straightforward: to explain the mechanical and chemical interactions between the two physical entities, foodstuff and organism, involved in nutrition. So, for example, we now know a great deal about that phosphorylation, the process by which the energy released by breaking down sugar and other foodstuffs is captured by the body's cells. As a serious scientist, Aristotle would welcome this new information. As just mentioned, however, for him nutritive activity cannot be adequately accounted for by the workings of two material components alone. It requires a third, the *psuchê*. In short, he rejects materialism, the view that only material objects—cells, sugars, proteins—exist, and thus refuses to confine his analysis of nutrition to the interactions between them.

Leon Kass, who agrees with Aristotle on this point—and so is willing to buck the general trend of contemporary biology—helpfully explains. The reductive analysis, he argues, while "illuminating, is not the whole story." By his lights, "more complex organisms cannot be understood as mere aggregates or sums of their component cells, even with respect to nourishment."[8] He explains in detail:

In a composition the so-called parts or elements are put together (*com + ponere*), "placed with" each other side by side, like bricks in a building or molecules in a crystal, without losing their individual identity. By contrast, in a concretion mutual interaction effects a *transformation* of the original subunits. The elements become "grown-together" (*con + cresco*) into a more intimate union, which submerges their original distinct identities into the larger whole.

When foodstuffs like sugars and fats become material for organic growth, self-maintenance or self-healing, their identity as discrete chemicals is submerged as they are *incorporated* into the larger units of life: cells, tissues, organs, organ systems, and finally, *the whole organism*.

Nourishing is thus the activity of self-renewal as well as self-fueling, self-maintenance, self-healing, and self-maturation. Its essence: the transformation of materials, from other to selfsame, *by the organism itself*—indeed by each of its cells, tissues, and organs, in well-coordinated and integrated processes of breakdown, biosynthesis and concretization—to preserve and to serve the organism as a living, performing whole.

Nourishing not only makes possible and sustains the performing whole; it is itself one of the whole's performances. As the many recent references to "self" imply, an organism feeds and nourishes *itself*. The impulse to feed, as well as all steps of ingestion, digestion, absorption, and regenerative biosynthesis, is an accomplishment of the animal itself. Though sustained by metabolism, an organism seems to be more than metabolism's product. It also appears to be its *cause*.

pp. 30–1 (my emphases)

Digesting food is not like adding another brick to a building. It is not merely the addition of stuff into a body. An animal is thus not a "composition," in which the parts composing the whole retain their identity. Instead, it is a "concretion," in which the nutrients added to the body lose their identity as they are transformed and incorporated into the whole. And the whole animal, the organism itself, is ultimately responsible for this taking place. Eating, as Kass makes wonderfully clear, is truly self-nourishment.

To clarify all this, focus on the word "whole." As we often say, it is more than the sum of its parts. A wooden table may have a flat top and four legs, but it is more than these five items. After all, if the legs were removed, the flat top put on the floor, and then the legs positioned upon it, the parts and their sum would remain the same. But there would no longer be a table, which must include a unifying pattern or ordering principle—a form that renders it a specific, a whole, piece of furniture.

Form is what makes a being a unity and a whole, in the world and through time. Form is that order or ordering that makes a one of the many components, giving it an integrity the components by themselves do not have. … Form provides not only unity but also specificity and identity.

Kass, p. 36

It is easy to conceive of a form when you think about a table, for it was made by a woodworker who had a specific idea in mind before she went to work on her material: the pile of lumber in the shop. This pile, however, could have been used to make a chair or a desk, as well as a table, for it was potentially all those things. But the woodworker wanted to make it into a table. To achieve this goal, she had to cut the lumber into pieces and then connect them in accord with her design. Doing this, she fashioned a whole from parts. She imposed form on the lumber, and at the end of the process an actual table in her shop was ready to be sold.

This example is straightforward. But what does it mean to talk, as both Aristotle and Kass do, about the form of an animal? Unlike a table, which received and then passively retained the woodworker's design, an animal is in continuous (metabolic) activity. As a result, its dimensions constantly fluctuate. Just weigh yourself on a precise scale ten times a day and, depending on how much you exercise, drink, and eat, you'll likely get ten different readings. Nonetheless, you persist as selfsame through time.

> Over the course of a lifetime of metabolizing, the organism persists, *though its materials do not*. Metabolism means the continuous exchange of stuff between inside and out, and no molecule in the organism is immune to turnover. Thus the organism is never the same materially, yet it persists as the same being, and indeed precisely by means of exchanging its materials.
>
> Kass, p. 41

An animal remains bounded, intact and thus distinct from, albeit continually dependent upon, its external environment. In fact, working to keep itself distinct from its immediate surroundings is the salient feature of a living being. This takes energy. Once that runs out, and the animal can work no longer, it will die, fall apart, decompose, and become indistinguishable from its environment. Retaining its integrity—from the Latin *integer*, "whole"—while alive is, says Kass, the achievement of its form, of itself. But unlike the static design or blueprint of a table,

> living form *is* generally *functioning* form or organization, that is, form in its work or activity just is this work. To be a something, to be a particular animal in the full sense, is to be that animal-at-work.
>
> p. 38

In Aristotelian terms, the *psuchê* is the form of an animal. In turn, the form is its "actuality." Two Greek words can be translated by this one English word: *energeia*, which literally means "being at work" and is the ancestor of our word "energy," and *entelecheia*. The latter is tricky. In its middle there is *telos*, which means "goal, end, or purpose." So *entelecheia* thus means something like "being in the state of having reached its goal." And the goal of a living being is to stay alive, intact and itself. In sum, *psuchê* as the "actuality" of a living body means something like "being at work keeping itself itself." Kass expresses this point more clearly:

This "persistence" and "independence" of form or organization is itself an achievement of form. The form of a given organism is a certain organization-in-action, whose first activity is to keep the enmattered organization-in-action (that is, itself) both organized and acting. The organization is not a mere outcome or heap or aggregate caused by the motions and joinings of the material parts. On the contrary, the joinings and motions of the material parts are caused and governed by the organization.

p. 42

Both Aristotle and Leon Kass reject materialism. For them, even the most primitive of life activities, self-nourishment, cannot be fully accounted for by the mechanical and chemical interactions between food and an organism's body. (Although, of course, the biologist is required to explain them.) They requires a third component to be added to the mix: the form of the animal, which, while inseparable from an animal's body, is not identical to it. Just as the whole is more than the sum of its parts—it must have, in addition, an ordering principle—so must an animal (or even a mushroom) have a *psuchê*, a living form, an "organization-in-action"—the whole organism at work nourishing itself, keeping itself alive; keeping itself itself.

> Even at a cellular level and even in the simplest organisms (for example, a bacterium or an amoeba), the sequence of chemical reactions is ordered and directed by structural and functional arrangements uniquely provided by the living cell: enzymes that catalyze the reactions; highly intricate three-dimensional intracellular structures (organelles), such as mitochondria or endoplasmic reticulum, that link chemical processes together that channel intermediates in functionally useful directions; positive and negative feedback mechanisms, which regulate the metabolic activity in keeping with the physiological needs of the cell and changes in its external environment; and so on. Moreover, the functional arrangements of molecules—in cell organelles, cells, tissues, organs, and organ systems—is the work not of the molecules as such. The living organization directs the comings and goings of molecules and all their interrelations, as the legislative guides the executive or a musical score the musicians. And organization, legislation and harmony, I remind you, are not themselves material.
>
> Kass, p. 42

There is nothing spiritual or mysterious about what Aristotle (or Kass) calls the *psuchê* (which is why "soul" is a bad choice for translating it here). Instead, it is "all the integrated vital powers of a naturally organic body, always possessed by such a body while it is alive" (Kass, p. 48). It is the whole organism keeping itself whole for as long as it can.

Unlike a materialist, Aristotle denies that we are just what we eat. On the other hand, unlike Socrates or Augustine, for him eating, and not of the metaphorical variety, is a fundamental aspect of what we are: animals. Even this, however, understates its importance for Aristotle. Eating, or what he calls the nutritive *psuchê*, provides him with a model by which two other characteristic features of human life, perception and thinking, can be understood. Shared by all organisms, eating is not only the most natural vital activity; it is also paradigmatic.

VI The Perceptive *Psuchê*

Perception, for Aristotle, is much like eating. This may sound odd because there is a huge difference between them. Having been eaten, an apple is incorporated into my body; it has been transformed and is no longer an apple. What remains within me, however, are only its material components (vitamins, minerals, sugars), while the apple itself, its form, is annihilated in the process. By contrast, sensible objects are neither transformed nor destroyed by my having perceived them, nor does their matter enter into my body. Instead, perception is a reception of "sensible forms" (424a18) without their matter. For this to occur there must be some distance between the perceiver and perceived. In Aristotelian terminology, "we perceive all things through a medium" (423b6).[9]

Despite this difference, nutrition and perception are deeply similar. To explain why, consider these two diagrams.[10]

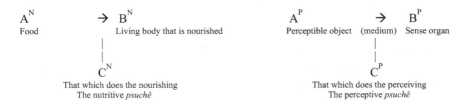

A^N → B^N A^P → B^P

Food   Living body that is nourished   Perceptible object   (medium)   Sense organ

C^N C^P

That which does the nourishing   That which does the perceiving
The nutritive *psuchê*   The perceptive *psuchê*

There is a structural parallel, or analogy, between eating and perceiving. In both, what is originally other and outside—food (A^N) and the perceptible object (A^P)—are received by, and become the same as, the living body (B^N) and the sense organ (B^P). In both, *psuchê* (C) is responsible for, is the cause of, the activity.

Consider a perceptual act. There is a brown door behind me, but I am not looking at it now. The door is, however, potentially visible, and so I can potentially see it. When I turn around, I will actually see it. When I do, I will receive the sensible form of the door. Because the light in my office is turned on, the transparent medium between me and the door (air) will be activated. The color of the door (its sensible form) will then energize the transparent medium and it will strike my eye. I will see the door and my eyes will undergo some physical change during the transition from the door being potentially visible to it becoming actually visible. As Aristotle puts it, "color moves the transparent medium, e.g., the air, and this, being continuous, acts upon the sense organ" (419a15).

The mechanics of this process are terribly difficult to explain, and would require a lecture on Aristotle's optics, itself a branch of physics. The salient point here, however, is only this: as with self-nourishment, vision cannot be reduced to the mechanical interactions between object and sense organ. It is a triadic, not a dyadic, activity, for it must include the *psuchê*. He explains why in the following, rather confusing, passage:

> We must understand as true generally of every sense that perception is the reception of sensible forms without matter. It is like wax, which receives the impression of the seal-ring without the iron or the gold. The wax receives the impact of the gold or bronze, but not as gold or bronze. It is similar when it comes to perception. The sense is affected by individual things that have color or flavor or sound, but not insofar as each of these is an individual, but insofar as each has a certain quality, and in accord with its *logos*. That in which this potentiality is primarily located is the sense organ. The potentiality and the sense organ are, on the one hand, the same; on the other hand, they are different. For the sense organ has magnitude, while neither sensing itself nor perception has magnitude. Instead, sensing is a *logos* and a potentiality.
>
> 424a16–28

To translate into simpler (and more contemporary) terminology: light hits the rose, which in turn reflects some of it toward my eyes, where it reaches my retina. Eventually it is transmitted to the brain through neuronal signaling, and I see a red rose. Aristotle's story is different, but it retains one key feature. My eyes are affected by seeing the red rose, but not just because the particular rose, understood as a physical and unique individual, affects it. Instead, my sense of sight is affected by the rose insofar as it has the quality of being red. In Aristotelian terms, it is affected "in accord with its *logos*," which here means "ratio." Because my eyes are constituted in a certain way (have certain proportions), they can receive, and then my nervous system can process, only a limited portion of the light reflected by the rose. What makes it possible for me to see, then, is not simply the material chunks of my eyes, or the red rose itself, but the *logos*, the specific structure or form of my visual apparatus, which allows it to receive a limited range of visual stimuli. If my eyes were to be physically changed (by, for example, staring directly into the sun), they would be thrown out of whack and would no longer function properly. For this reason, Aristotle concludes, a sense such as vision cannot be reduced to the physical sense organ, the eye, and perceiving cannot be fully accounted for by the mechanical interactions of object and sense organ. Instead, a sense such as vision is "a kind of ratio and potentiality" (424a25). Just as with self-nutrition, what is ultimately responsible for perception, its cause, is the *psuchê*, the *logos* or form of the sense organ.

To explain the details of this theory is far too large a task, and so I will again concentrate only on the issue relevant here: the manner in which perception is like eating. To do so, consider what can be called Aristotle's "realism." By his lights, there are mind-independent objects out there in the world—things that do not require us to think about them in order to exist—and human beings can perceive them as they really are in themselves. You ask me, how is the honey? I respond, it is sweet. This is the right answer because, on the realist's view, the honey really is sweet and my sensory apparatus accurately has detected it as such.

However commonsensical such realism may seem, it is radically out of date. Consider the following passage written by Galileo some four hundred years ago:

> I think, therefore, that these tastes, odors, colors, etc., so far as their objective existence is concerned, are nothing but mere names for something that resides exclusively in our sensitive body, so that if the perceiving creatures were removed, all of these qualities would be annihilated and abolished from existence.[11]

According to Galileo, the honey is not really sweet. Instead, like all physical objects it is no more than a conglomerate of particles, which have no "secondary qualities" like sweet or hot or red, at all. The only qualities they do have are "primary" (and quantitative) ones like velocity, magnitude, and shape. When physical objects interact with our sensory apparatus, itself also composed of particles, and our nervous system is activated, and our brain registers those stimuli and we somehow become conscious of them, the results are sensations of qualities like sweet or hot or red. These qualities, however, do not exist independently in the external object but instead reside, as Galileo puts it, "exclusively in our sensitive body"—largely in our brains. We say, and it sure tastes like, the honey is sweet. It may seem so, but it is not really. For honey is no more than nonsweet particles in motion, and the sensation of sweetness we experience is the result of the interaction between them and those composing my body. On this view, human beings and their perceptions are encased in a kind of neurological bubble that keeps them one step removed from the external world. On this view, familiar statements such as "the rose is red" and "the wind is cold" are fundamentally misleading.

Aristotle's story is different. He is a secondary quality realist, which is to say he begins by trusting our ordinary perceptions, and our ordinary statements about them. For him, the rose really is red, the boiling water is hot, and so when we perceive them as such, we get things right. Precisely for this reason, perceiving is like eating. Just as we eat food, which really exists out there in the world, and successfully make it the same as ourselves through digestion, so too do human beings successfully perceive things in the world for what they really are. Just as food becomes identical to the body, if only in matter, so too does a sensible object become identical to the sense, if only in form. In both cases what is external and other becomes internal and same. By contrast, for Galileo, whose view is now fully ensconced in the contemporary field of neuroscience, our sensory lives are sundered from the world as it really is. The rose, the one out there in the world, is essentially different from the rose as I perceive it. It is not red.

This line of thought, in which the nutritive and perceptive *psuchê* are analogous, has one grand implication. Human beings are like other animals in one decisive respect: we are at home in the world. We have our niche, a nourishing place, around which we can find our way by seeing, hearing, smelling, touching, tasting, and eating what is outside of us. While the Aristotelian stance toward perception, our most basic way of encountering the external world, is trust, the modern view, inaugurated by scientists like Galileo, is suspicion or even contempt.

The modern view, at least according to Nietzsche, originated with Socrates, "the one turning point and vortex of so-called world history." Supremely optimistic about the power of human reason, he located humanity's true calling in the erotic drive to discover eternal truth. To succeed in this task, he demanded that we separate ourselves as far as possible from our bodies and their many distractions. For Socrates, then, we are anything but at home in the world. His pernicious otherworldliness was then radicalized by his infernal progeny: the Christian for whom our true home, and only hope, is not here, but in the eternal beyond.

By contrast, Aristotle is a philosopher with his feet planted firmly on the ground. He takes us to be animals. His worldliness is manifested most directly in his understanding of *psuchê*. It is not immaterial "soul" but the life principle at work in every organism. Its primordial manifestation is self-nourishment, and every subsequent (more developed) activity, such as perception, is grounded on, and so takes its bearings from, the "nutritive *psuchê*." As such, Aristotle seems now to be firmly aligned with Homer, and his worldview thus seems to allow the possibility of a good dinner party becoming a worthy and meaningful endeavor. After all, no other activity more immediately activates our animality, so why not celebrate it as such?

VII The Generation of Animals

Aristotle's "primary" *psuchê* is responsible not only for self-nourishment but also for sexual reproduction. The story here, though, becomes a bit strange.

> The nutritive *psuchê* belongs to all animals, and is the first and most common power of *psuchê*, in virtue of which they all have life. Its tasks are generation and incorporating nutrients. For this is the most natural of all animal activity: … the making of another like itself; an animal an animal, a plant a plant, in order that they might have a share as far as possible in what lasts forever and the divine. For all living things strive for that and do what they naturally do for the sake of that.
>
> 415a26–b3

This description of generation (from the Latin *generare*, "bring forth, beget, produce") is, perhaps jarringly, rather similar to the one Socrates, through the voice of Diotima, offers in the *Symposium*. Eros there is characterized as "love of immortality," and as a drive found in all animals. In the vast majority of them, it is manifested simply in the urge to reproduce. Haven't you noticed, she asks Socrates,

> the terrible condition all the beasts, both footed and winged, are in whenever they desire to generate? They are all sick and in the grip of Eros. This is found first in their desire for sexual intercourse, then in their desire to nourish their offspring. Indeed, the weakest of them are prepared to battle the stronger, even to die, on behalf of their offspring, and they will endure hunger themselves, and do anything, in order to nourish them.
>
> 207a7–b6

Animals go wild in mating season and fight to the death to protect their young. Even if they are unaware of being so, they are animated by Eros, the love of immortality, and the only way for a mortal being to achieve this is metaphorical: through the generation of another like itself, which will live on in the future after the parent has died. We might tolerate such an explanation from Socrates, who in his own way is quite mad. But surely we expect a more sober analysis from Aristotle, the zoologist par excellence. Nonetheless, he too declares that all living beings strive for what is immortal and divine. Still, despite its Socratic echo, his story is meant to be scientific, and to give a naturalistic explanation of a set of observable facts.

Every organism is impelled to extend itself, both as an individual and as a member of a species, into the future. It accomplishes the first task through nutrition, by which it persists as itself—retains its form—and the second through generation, in which the species (*eidos*) lives on even as the individual dies. The best explanation, Aristotle thinks, of this, the futurity of all living beings, is their striving to be immortal. In the passage above, he does not use Socrates' word "eros." Instead, his term is *orexis*, "urge" or "drive," which naturalizes what for Socrates could be construed as a spiritual force. In Aristotle's view, the striving for what is divine and free from death accounts for the way animals sacrifice themselves for their offspring and plants stretch themselves toward the sun to gather nourishing light.

In his treatise *The Generation of Animals*, Aristotle elaborates a bit. Of all existing things, he says, some are eternal and divine. They neither come nor cease to be. Others, however, are temporary; they first come to be and then cease to be. Eternal beings, he thinks, are ontologically superior to transitory ones. Among the latter, however, some are better, others worse. Most important, living beings are better than inanimate things. Plants are better than rocks. This is so because even though every particular organism dies, it participates in the eternal "specifically"; it reproduces its species in its offspring. The form lives on after the individual organism ceases to be. (And for Aristotle, unlike Darwin, species are permanent features of the biological landscape.) Form is ontologically superior to matter; *psuchê*, even if inseparable from body, is thus superior to it. Since all living beings strive both to nourish themselves, and thereby to keep themselves intact, and to reproduce themselves—to extend their species into the next generation—all are ultimately striving for form.

With this line of thought, one must now wonder: Has Aristotle's thinking successfully purged itself of Socratic otherworldliness? Or are these passages a residue of what he imbibed when he studied with Plato for twenty years? To reiterate the guiding question of this chapter, is his view closer to that of Homer or to that of Socrates?

VIII Aristotle's Intellect

In his book the *Nicomachean Ethics*, Aristotle addresses the question, what is human happiness? He begins with a straightforward observation. Every human action and choice "seems to aim at some good" (1094a3).[12] Except when we are overpowered by external forces (such as the wind blowing us around), the moves we make are intentional, purposive, for a reason. We pursue our objectives, our ends or goals, because we think it is good to do so. (Sadly, we are often quite wrong about this.)

The next step in his argument: the goods or ends we pursue are ordered hierarchically. I walk to the store in order to buy milk, which is the end or goal (*telos*) of my walk, and why I got up from my chair and left the house. When I bring it home I will drink it. A teleological sequence has emerged: walking is for the sake of buying milk; buying milk is for the sake of drinking it. Such is the progression of our lives, which is like a ladder whose rungs are composed of means leading to ends, which in turn become means to something else. We pursue A in order to achieve B, which is "higher" than A. In turn this will lead us to C, which is "higher" than both B and A.

The next question: Does the ladder have a highest rung? In other words, does the sequence in which an end becomes a means to achieve a higher end ever come to a halt? Is there, in other words, a "highest good" (1094a23), a final end, which we desire only for itself rather than because it leads us to something else? If there were not, the sequence would "go on infinitely." But, Aristotle states, if this were the case, then "our desire would be futile and pointless" (1094a22). All our actions and pursuits would be for the sake of something else, and since the sequence would be infinite everything we did would not advance us upward in any meaningful sense. A ladder with no final rung is no ladder at all. A may be for the sake of B, and B for the sake of C, but if the sequence just keeps going, then C would be no closer to an end than B. Nothing would ultimately matter more than anything else, and so all our strivings would be meaningless. Therefore, he concludes, the sequence cannot be infinite. As he puts it, "there exists an end in the realm of action which we desire for its own sake ... this is the highest good" (1094a16–23).

This argument has an obvious gap. Aristotle must here be presupposing that desire is not futile and pointless. But why does he think this, and why did he not make this premise explicit? Perhaps because he takes it to be so obvious that he does not even need to mention it. And this is because he is at heart a biologist.

In dissecting an animal's corpse in order to study its anatomy, a zoologist assumes that everything she finds must have a function and contribute something to the maintenance of the organism as a whole. Similarly, an entomologist observing bees will assume there is a reason behind every one of their flights. Animated by just such a conviction, Aristotle finds it inconceivable that human desire and action are pointless. Like other animals, everything we do has a point. Plugging this implicit assumption into the argument above, it leads to the proposition that the sequence of means and ends cannot be infinite. (If it were infinite, then life itself would become pointless; which it is not.) In turn, this leads to the conclusion that there must be a highest good, an end in itself.

And what might this be? Happiness (*eudaimonia*). Unlike everything else, we do not seek it in order to gain anything other than itself. Its value is intrinsic, not instrumental. Or, as Aristotle puts it, happiness is "self-sufficient," which means that "taken by itself it makes life desirable" (1097b15).

Virtually everyone, he believes, would agree with him on this, and he may be right. If I were to ask you, "What do you ultimately want?" you likely would answer, "To be happy." And why do you want to be happy? Your response likely would be, "Because I want to be happy." Period. But even if Aristotle is right, it is hardly obvious what this means. As he puts it, "to call happiness the highest good is perhaps a little trite" (1097b23). His next task, then, is to elucidate its nature. Without explaining why, he commences his investigation with this suggestion: "Perhaps this is best done by first ascertaining the unique function (*ergon*) of human being" (1097b24).

"What can this function possibly be?" he then asks. "Simply living? [Human beings] share that even with plants, but we are now looking for something peculiar to human beings." Could it be "the life of nutrition and growth" or "a life of sense perception? But we have these in common with the horse, the ox, and every animal" (1097b30–1098a3).

Aristotle is on the hunt for the special activity or work or function that distinguishes human animals as a species. As a zoologist, he is convinced there must be one. After all, "there seems to be a specific function of the eye, hand, and foot" (1097b31), and if this is true of the parts of an organism's body, so too, he reasons, must it hold of the animal as a whole.[13] Just as (to offer an oversimplified example) what makes an eagle an eagle, and different from a shark, is its ability to fly high and fast, so can every animal be distinguished by capacities unique to its species. For this reason, Aristotle rejects nutrition and perception, which are shared by all animals, as the specific work of human beings. Instead, he offers this: "There remains then an active life of the rational element" (*logos*: 1098a3). Or, as he puts it in another treatise, we are the only animals who "have *logos*" (*Politics*, 1253a9). No other, he thinks, can reason, think, argue, ask questions, seek explanations, engage in scientific inquiry. "The peculiar function of human beings, then, consists in an activity (*energeia*) of the *psuchê* in accord with *logos*" (1098a8).

Having taken this as a biological fact, Aristotle believes he has laid the foundation for his account of *eudaimonia*, which he now defines as "activity (*energeia*) of the *psuchê* in accord with excellence or virtue (*aretê*)" (1098a18). Happiness is a life spent in sustained, excellent rational work. As opposed to the way we typically construe it today, it is not just feeling good about oneself. It is not, in other words, simply a subjective or first-person experience. Because it is found in the maximal activation of the distinctive feature of humanity, our capacity to reason, it can be objectively determined. Just as an ornithologist would describe an eagle with a deformed wing as deficient, so would Aristotle describe a human being who does little by way of rational work, regardless of the way he feels about himself, as less than happy. By now it should come as no surprise that the Greek word he uses, *eudaimonia*, is not perfectly captured by our "happiness." Other possible translations include "well-being" and "flourishing." *Eudaimonia* is the supremely healthy, maximally energized life, experienced by people who have become most fully themselves. And this is, he argues, the highest good, the *telos* for which we all strive.

Aristotle's is a biologically informed ethics. On the one hand, this would, yet again, seem to place him firmly in Homer's camp. But the story gets complicated. After all, what makes us unique among the animals is our innate ability to engage in *logos*. Therefore, what constitutes the best human life, and makes us truly happy, is the sustained activation of this capacity. With this idea, however, Aristotle seems to be inching closer to Socrates. Reasoning and philosophizing, rather than eating and drinking, are the paradigmatic manifestations of our humanity, and what we do when we are at our best. What makes us the animals we are is precisely what makes us least like the rest of them.

He makes this point at the end of his *Nicomachean Ethics*. Here he argues that the best of all possible lives, the one bringing "complete happiness," is found in theoretical activity. For this, he says, is the best work of what is best in us, namely "intellect" (*nous*: 1177a17–20), the dimension of the *psuchê* responsible for thinking and reasoning—for *logos*. Such work, he argues, is the most reliable, continuous, pleasant, and self-sufficient activity available to human beings. It "alone seems to be liked because of itself alone" (1177b1); it offers no reward other than itself. Theoretical activity, the maximal energizing of our rational capacity, has all the features Aristotle identified as belonging to the highest good.

He culminates this line of thought in a most surprising, because distinctly Socratic, way:

> Such a life might exceed the human. For one lives this way not insofar as one is a human being, but insofar as something divine belongs to him. The extent to which [the theoretical life] differs from the life of the [psychosomatic] compound is the same as that to which the excellent activation of it [*nous*]

compares to other kinds of excellence. Indeed, if intellect is divine compared to the human, so too is the theoretical life divine compared to the human life. Thus one should not, as the saying goes, "think human things because one is a human being, nor mortal things because one is mortal," but as far as possible one should strive to be immortal and do everything in life with an eye to what is best in us. For even if it [intellect] is small in bulk, its power and value is much greater than everything else. In fact, it would seem that each one of us simply is this [intellect], if it is authoritative and best.

1177b26–35

In theoretical activity, the maximal activation of intellect, a thinker apprehends and in this sense makes contact with the permanent principles, the formal structures, of the world, and thereby distances himself from the essential feature of animality: its transience. Such it is to become, however metaphorically, "divine."

The "saying" Aristotle mentions in this passage above echoes some lines from the *Bacchae* quoted in Chapter 2. The chorus, filled with foreboding at Pentheus' catastrophic desire to suppress Dionysus, offers him a warning:

Unwise are those who aspire,
who outrange the limits of man.
Briefly, we live. Briefly,
then die. Wherefore, I say,
he who hunts a glory, he who tracks
some boundless, superhuman dream,
may lose his harvest here and now
and garner death. Such men are mad,
their counsels evil.

394–403

Like Socrates, Aristotle seems to reject such down-to-earth counsel. Be a god, he urges his reader, as far as you can! Which is to say, philosophize with all your might. If this means forgoing the pleasures of the dinner table, so be it. In fact, in his paean to the theoretical life, Aristotle denigrates "other kinds of excellence." What he has in mind are practical or ordinary virtues such as justice, courage, moderation, or generosity, all of which require us to act especially well in our relations with other people and in our communities. These he discusses at great length in earlier chapters of the *Nicomachean Ethics*, where he seems to affirm them as first-rate actualizations of human possibility. By contrast, when the book draws to a close, he seems to denigrate them in favor of the extraordinary life of theoretical activity. The passage thus recalls Socrates' speech in the *Symposium*. In ascending upward on the erotic ladder, the philosopher looks down with contempt on its lower rungs. In a similar fashion, Aristotle describes those many people who hold bodily pleasures in high esteem as "slavish" and more like "fatted cattle" (1095b20) than genuinely human beings. Even if, like all animals, we nourish ourselves, sexually reproduce, and care for our offspring, we are unique. For we have *logos* and thus are aware of, and capable of transcending, our own animality. We can philosophize, and only in doing so can we achieve the *telos* of our species and thereby fully become ourselves. This, however, requires us to touch upon the divine. Paradoxically, then, the fullest expression of our humanity requires us to cease being human.

Once again, we are reminded of Socrates, who, in the *Phaedo*, described the philosopher as engaged in the practice of death and dying. But this is a jarring way to think about Aristotle. While Socrates was utterly untroubled, even bemused, at the prospect of his own death, Aristotle must have hated to die. He loved life and the world, and he wanted to study all of it. On his deathbed he surely must have been pained by the fact that he had more work to do, more forms to investigate.

Who, then, is Aristotle, and what kind of life is this, anyway?

IX Is the *Psuchê* Immortal?

Book II of *De Anima* began with a study of self-nutrition, the most natural of all vital activities. These chapters accentuated the continuity of human beings with other organisms, and so *psuchê* as used there should be translated as "life principle" rather than "soul." After all, even a tree has a *psuchê*. Just as it strives to maintain its individual form through nutrition, and extend its species into the future through reproduction, so do we. Aristotle's story moved next to perception, the vital capacity possessed by all animals. The third major segment of *De Anima* concerns "the part of *psuchê* by which it thinks and knows" (419a10), namely intellect (*nous*). Here Aristotle, who earlier had proclaimed, "One need no more ask whether *psuchê* and body are one than whether the wax and impression are one," now asks whether intellect might in fact be "separable" (429a11). If it is, then the rigorous naturalism (worldliness) pervading *De Anima* may well be severely disrupted by its account of human thinking. If it is, then perhaps *psuchê* should be translated as "soul."

What, for Aristotle, is thinking? On the one hand, it is analogous to perceiving. The latter is a reception of sensible forms. The perceptive faculty "is potentially like the perceptible object [in form] even though it is not the perceptible object," and it becomes actually like the object in the sensory act. In a similar fashion, the intellect is receptive of "intelligible objects" (*noêta*: 429a18). But there are huge differences as well. First, while an animal can apprehend only a limited range of sensible forms (a range of sounds, say), intellect can think anything. And while vision, for example, cannot take place without the presence of an external and potentially visible thing (and some light), intelligible objects do not need to be physically present for us to think. I can think about Socrates or Italy or dinner anywhere and anytime I want. Finally, a sensory organ will be degraded or rendered inoperative by excessive stimulation. A terribly loud sound will damage my hearing, and a too bright light will diminish my ability to see. By contrast, "when intellect thinks the extremely intelligible it is no less capable of thinking what is less intelligible. In fact, it can do so even more" (429b5).

To reformulate: whether we perceive an object is not entirely up to us, since the object actually has to be there, and to be of the right sort and in the right conditions, for our sensory apparatus to apprehend it. But no such constraints obtain for the intellect. For thinking somehow takes place within us. To clarify, recall the diagrams sketched earlier.

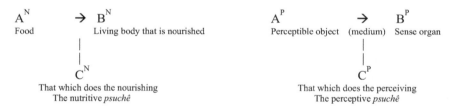

Both nutrition and perception have a triadic structure. A^N is a foodstuff. Actually unlike the living body which will eat it (B^N), but potentially like it, it exists outside the body until it is digested and made actually identical with the body (if only in matter). Analogously, the sensible object (A^P), before it is perceived, is actually unlike but potentially like the sense organ (B^P). When it is sensed it becomes actually like, if only in form. Finally, an analysis of both self-nutrition and perceiving requires a third element, the *psuchê* (C), which is ultimately responsible for the activity taking place.

Thinking too has a triadic structure. When intelligible objects are thought by the intellect, they (like sensible objects and food) transition from being actually unlike, but potentially like, to being actually like. Actual knowledge, the highest form of thinking, is, Aristotle says, "the same as the object" (430a20). Like perceiving and eating, thinking is a vital activity by which other becomes same, and *psuchê* is responsible for this transition taking place. But the difference has already been mentioned: an intelligible object is not physically out there in the world existing independently. After all, we can summon a thought—about trees or numbers or anything else—whenever and wherever we want. The consequence of this simple observation is monumental. Unlike vision, which requires healthy eyes, or hearing, which requires ears, intellect does not have a bodily organ. If it did, then, like hearing and seeing, it too would suffer a corresponding restriction. However, since intellect "thinks everything," it cannot be restricted at all. Indeed, it is nothing but the potential to think everything, and so "is nothing in actuality before it thinks" (429a24). It "must be unmixed" (429a17) with no specific physical components. The upshot: unlike the nutritive and perceptive *psuchê*, "intellect is separable [from the body]" (439b6).

Intelligible objects must somehow be in the intellect. More specifically, they are in what Aristotle calls the "passive intellect" (*pathetikeos nous*: 430a34), which he describes as like "the place of forms" (429a27). Furthermore, as in perception and self-nourishment, thinking requires an agent (C) responsible for the transition from potentiality to actuality (from A to B) taking place. Intellect, then, must be more than just passive.

> Since in all of nature, indeed in every kind of being, there is matter (which is potentiality in every thing), and another which is the active cause and causes everything … there must be such differences in the *psuchê*. So the intellect is both such as to become all things and to cause all things.
>
> 429a10–16

Roughly sketched, thinking now looks like this.

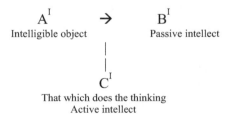

A^I → B^I
Intelligible object   Passive intellect

C^I
That which does the thinking
Active intellect

However analogous this triadic structure may be to those found in self-nourishment and perception, there is a monumental difference, for the entire operation takes place within the intellect. The intelligible object (A^I) is somehow already in the passive intellect (B^I), which is potentially all things and no particular thing in actuality until it thinks. And the active intellect (C^I) is somehow the cause of the transition from potentiality to actuality.[14] Hence, the active intellect, which has no physical component, is "separate" from the body. Pushing this idea even further, Aristotle next declares it to be "immortal and everlasting" (430a22). But how in the world, if "*psuchê* and body are one"—as Aristotle so adamantly avers in Book II—could this be possible?

Strangely, he does not elaborate. Perhaps he knows he is in a conceptual thicket from which smooth extrication is simply not available.[15]

X What Is Knowing?

To approach this thicket from another direction, consider the first chapter of *The Metaphysics*. Here Aristotle traces the steps through which human beings acquire knowledge. The first is perception, the faculty we share with all other animals, and which affords us access to real (mind-independent) objects standing outside of our bodies. Next comes memory, which somehow preserves those perceptions. Not all animals have it, but those that do are "more intelligent and capable of learning than those not capable of remembering" (980b20). After memory comes what he calls "experience," which in Greek is *empeiria* (the root of "empirical"). This seems to be an accumulation and grouping of particular memories into some sort of unified clumps. So, to update Aristotle's own illustrative example, when I had a headache two weeks ago, I took an aspirin and then quickly felt better. When my friend Bob was suffering from a headache, I remembered what had happened to me, and so I gave him an aspirin, and it alleviated his pain. When another friend suffered from a similar problem, I also urged him to take one. He did, and again the pain went away. Now, should someone approach me with the same complaint, I will confidently make the same recommendation, which may well work again. I am now "experienced" in the use of aspirin.

Still, I am far from having real knowledge, for this requires more than a recognition that aspirin has been successful in the past, and a confident belief that it is likely to work in the future. It requires an explanation, a *logos*, of why this is so.

Consider the difference between a veteran nurse and a young physician. The former has treated a vast number of patients and, because he has a sharp mind and a strong memory and his many years in the field have taught him to recognize the specific needs of individuals, he can quickly identify a set of symptoms and correctly predict the proper course of treatment. The latter has had an extensive scientific education, and so is able to explain how a drug works and why it is effective in treating a specific disease. She has real knowledge of the chemical processes at work when, for example, aspirin enters the human bloodstream. At the same time, however, she may have precious little experience with, or interest in, particular human beings. Her knowledge has largely come from books, classrooms, and laboratories. In such circumstances, the nurse may actually be superior to the physician in treating individual patients. Aristotle says as much.

> When it comes to getting things done, experience seems to differ little from knowledge. Indeed, we see people with experience frequently succeeding better than those who can give a *logos* but have little in the way of experience. The reason for this is that experience is familiarity with particulars, while knowledge is of universals, and all actions and effects take place among particulars. ... So if someone has a *logos* without experience, he may often make mistakes in his treatment.
>
> 981a12–17

Nonetheless, the physician, Aristotle thinks, is "wiser" (981a25) than, and ultimately superior to, the nurse. Not only does she know that aspirin works in alleviating the pain of a headache, but she also can explain, without referring to any particular patient, why it does so. She knows the cause. Thus, although the nurse treats his patients quite well, he is restricted to the level of experience, which in turn is dependent upon the accumulation and organization of particular memories. And so Aristotle speaks rather disparagingly of him, regardless of how efficacious he may be. He compares the person with only experience to an "inanimate object which acts without knowledge of what it is doing" (981b4). Because human beings are the animals with *logos*, our best selves emerge not through practical success but in being able to answer "why" questions; in knowing causes, forms, universals; in becoming wise.

Still, even if knowledge is genuinely superior to experience, "in human beings, knowledge and science emerge through experience" (981a3). Because experience itself emerges from memories, which in turn originate in perceptions, science originates in perceptions. But here's the rub: How can knowledge of universals arise from perception, which is of particulars? On the one hand, it may seem relatively easy to answer this question: from induction and empirical generalization. An example: because temperatures in Boston have been recorded for many decades, it is possible to predict with a high degree of confidence that the temperature in any given February will not reach eighty degrees Fahrenheit. This sort of empirical generalization is both useful and relatively reliable.

Aristotle, however, credits induction with a more substantial achievement. He tries to explain:

> It is impossible to think about universals except by induction … and impossible to induce without perception. For it is perception that is of particulars: it is not possible to get understanding of these. Indeed [one cannot get understanding] of universals without induction, and induction is impossible without perception.[16]

Aristotelian induction not only issues in a probabilization based upon the generalization of many particular cases, it actually provides the epistemic resources for making universal, scientific claims. How it does so, however, is not clear. The statement, "the temperature does not exceed eighty degrees in Boston in February," while sounding like a firm and universal claim, is not really that. After all, while it is unlikely that it will exceed eighty degrees in February, it is not impossible. This claim, then, does not seem to reach the level of intellectual rigor required by a genuine science, whose content (according to Aristotle) must be real universals and necessary truth. But necessary truth is not available in perception, memory, or experience, the components of induction. There thus seems to be a gap in Aristotle's account of how we acquire scientific knowledge. It is just not clear how the human mind moves from the particulars to universals.

Perhaps he addresses this gap in the following, rather cryptic, statement he makes in the *Posterior Analytics*: "One perceives a particular, but perceiving is of the universal. So, for example, we perceive a human being, not Callias, a human being" (*Posterior Analytics*, 100b1).

Imagine you are in an elevator. You glance to your right and see someone wearing a large coat, a hat, and sunglasses. After you have exited, I ask, "Who was in the elevator standing next to you?" Since you could identify almost none of the person's individual features, not even gender, all you could say is, "A person." You recognized a human being, but that's about it. Now, suppose that instead of an unidentifiable person, your friend Callias happened to be standing next to you in the elevator. If I asked you, "Whom did you see?" you would answer, "Callias." But were you to answer either "a man" or "a person," these too would also qualify as correct answers. The point is this: we never see raw individuals. All particular things are also instances of more general kinds. I see this table, and it is both a unique object made forty years ago as well as a member of a category: tables. In fact, it is a member of an even larger category: pieces of furniture. So, if you ask me, "What is underneath your laptop?" I can give you at least three correct answers: the table in my living room made forty years ago, a table, a piece of furniture. The object under my laptop is not simply a unique individual. Just like the thing in your living room, it is a table.

When we perceive, we see, hear, taste, smell, or touch two things at once: the individual object close at hand and what kind of object it is. I see Callias and a human being, the species to which he belongs, at the same time. In short, the universal is in the particular, and so is there to be seen.

All animals have perception. The vast majority have memory, and many also have a share of experience. A lion seeing an individual zebra moves toward it because it recognizes a familiar and welcome source of food. It sees its prey both as an individual and as a member of a species, which is why it hunts it rather than the elephant standing nearby. Unlike a human being, however, the lion cannot transcend the cognitive level of experience and achieve scientific knowledge. It cannot study zoology. Nor does it need to, for it is able to hunt the zebra just fine. As Aristotle said, "we see people with experience frequently succeeding better than those who can give a *logos* but have little in the way of experience." Lions are better at hunting than most zoologists, but the latter are wiser. They can explain why, for example, big cats have evolved as they have and can now hunt as well as they do. Human beings have the capacity to reflect upon, process, and develop the proto-universals stored up in experience (which in turn emerge from perception and memory) and transform them into the genuine universals which constitute science. They can do so because even in the rudimentary act of seeing a particular, the universal was, albeit latently, present.

Another example: Many people have had ample experience with dogs. Because they have had so many nice encounters with these friendly animals, they like them a lot and will gladly approach a new one when they encounter it on the street. A person with a great deal of experience with many different kinds of dogs can even become an accomplished trainer able to assist others in molding their pet into an obedient and reliable companion. Finally, some dog trainers might become extremely interested in what makes dogs tick. Why, they ask, are these animals so easy to train, while others, such as wolves, are not? Answering this question requires a foray into zoology. The dog likely evolved from the gray wolf many thousands of years ago and became a different species entirely. Quite unlike a wolf, however, a dog has a keen sense of hierarchy and will submit to the top dog. Dogs rarely cooperate with other members of their own species. Wolves, by contrast, work together well in packs in ways dogs do not. Why this is so can be explained by the evolutionary biologist, and so the dog trainer, eager to learn, enrolls in a graduate program in zoology where he studies universal features of both wolves and dogs. The transition from experience to science has been made. Knowledge emerged from but went beyond experience. Again, all of this is made possible by the fact that the universal was latent in the perceptible particular.

Whether this sort of sketch can be successfully fleshed out—whether, in other words, Aristotle's empiricism can be substantiated as a viable theory of knowledge acquisition—remains to be seen. Still, this much is clear. He views the human encounter with the world as operating on two levels simultaneously: the particular and the universal. We perceive individual form-matter conglomerates—this lion running after that zebra—and we think about intelligible forms or universals. Other animals do something like this as well. The lion sees not only a zebra over there but also a member of a general category and thus a recognizable source of food. Human beings bring this feature of animal life to a higher, more reflective level. We become scientists who study universals, formulate theories, and, if successful, articulate the truth about the world. The process may begin with a blunt encounter with particulars in perception, but it ends with universal knowledge and a theoretical *logos*. Such, at least, are the outlines of Aristotle's story.

XI The Fractured *Psuchê*

The previous sections were risky, for they broached (and oversimplified) some of the most difficult topics Aristotle addresses, ones that have preoccupied scholars for millennia. The risk, though, was worth taking if only for one reason: in order to formulate a proposal. Aristotle's conception of human life is unsettling. In the early chapters of *De Anima*, *psuchê* is conceived in thoroughly naturalized terms, is said to be inseparable from the body, and so, as in the *Odyssey*, means "principle of life." Here he seems to embrace our animality full bore. Later, however, when he discusses intellect (*nous*), *psuchê* becomes separable, immortal, and thus better rendered as "soul." Yes, he seems to be saying, we are animals, but unlike the rest of them we have *logos*, the capacity for rational activity, and our intellects can propel us beyond. Similarly, at the close of the *Nicomachean Ethics* he identifies happiness with theoretical activity, which he construes as nearly divine. At the end of both books, then, he sounds less like the down-to-earth zoologist and more like the Socrates of the *Symposium* and *Phaedo*, according to whom we only become genuinely ourselves by transcending our flesh and blood.

Many a commentator has concluded that Aristotle's writings are simply not consistent, and it is easy to see why. Still, while it may not be possible to extract from them a smooth and untroubled story, they are, taken as a whole, wonderfully coherent. However conflicting they may appear, they combine to offer a faithful depiction of human experience. For we are conflicted beings. As animals, we eat, drink, and sexually reproduce. Our feet stand firmly on the ground (for a little while), and we live with family, friends, and strangers, with whom we gladly share our food and wine. As animals with intellect and *logos*, however, we distance ourselves from both others and ourselves. We find the world interesting, puzzling, questionable. We wonder about it, and thus begin to seek wisdom. We recognize patterns, see forms, hunt down universals, formulate theories. In doing so, we separate ourselves from the warm bodies surrounding us and, like Socrates, may well find eating and drinking, cooking and cleaning the dishes, no more than a tiresome burden.

Books like the *Nicomachean Ethics* and *De Anima* end surprisingly, and seemingly at odds with their prior chapters, not because they are confused or suffer from faulty logic. Instead, they tell the difficult truth about the human condition. We are fractured beings, suspended somewhere in between particular and universal, animal and god. As a result, the place of food and drink in our lives is vexed. On the one hand, we should be grateful for our time together at the dinner table, for here, as Homer teaches so well, we find our most honest, and best, selves. Taking the time to cook, and then to pour wine, and to share it all with others, is an affirmation of who we are. Next to nothing, but not nothing. On the other hand, as Socrates reminds us, we are creatures restless at our core, with an urge to learn as much as we can about the formal structures of the world we inhabit. The task is inexhaustible, and to it we should dedicate the little time we have to it. On this view, food and wine take a back seat to the hard, but finally most rewarding, work of philosophy.

So which is it? Are eating and drinking genuinely valuable activities in themselves, or are they, at best, metaphors to express the consumption of ideas? Aristotle, I propose, wants it both ways. He is willing to confront our fractured natures with open eyes, and for this reason he is the (uncomfortable) hero of this book.

Postlude

(36)

My best intoxications have come not from wine but from speaking in front of a large group of students. If it goes really well, as it only occasionally does, the rushing stream of my consciousness, usually under tight control, comes to the surface. I read a passage out loud, and then illustrate it with an example, and then thoughts, memories, stories gallop by, flow rapidly and without hesitation. I am a responsible teacher and so I resist self-indulgence. Most of the time, when I manage to crack the students up, I pull back, not wanting to get sucked into the gratifying vortex of their laughter. But every once in a while, I just let loose. Even without wine, a touch of madness and my tongue loosens. Winged words fly, and there are a few young people in the room who might even be listening. What could be better?

If only I could write the way I speak on those occasions. But I am also all too responsible at the keyboard. I feel a duty to the texts on which I offer comment. I am, finally, a professional explainer.

(37)

Managed to score a bag of honeycrisp apples at the market on Sunday. The farmer was just giving them away because most were soft and compromised by age. Like me. Gina's thinking apple crisp, which would be nice. I'm thinking sauce. Chop them up, add some orange juice, blend with a tablespoon or two of horseradish.

Can't get excited about making dinner at home. Would have to be a pasta with pecorino Romano and pepper, or a roast and an industrial salad. We have a few watermelon radishes and some carrots from last weeks' indoor market, but this hardly gets my heart beating.

(38)

Gina and I decide we'll walk to Glenville Stops for dinner, even though it's cold and windy outside. A quiet, comfortable bar, run by an English guy. Excellent beer selection. I imagine myself ordering the steak frites, simple and satisfying if you're hungry, which I am. But it's too early to leave, so I start to drink. I open a bottle of Valpolicella. A straightforward wine, modestly priced, from Verona. Francesco gave his approval a few weeks ago, and I've been buying bottles whenever I walk past my local shop. I knock down a large glass quickly. I turn on some music. Tuareg musicians from the Sahara Desert. Getting tipsy, just want to float a bit with the tunes. Lots on my mind, mostly flits emerging from this book, and they flow without much abrasion.

I wonder, is Aristotle the hero of this book? He does better justice to the human split than anyone else. The animal with *logos*. How perfect is that? We are born, breathe, eat, excrete, generate, die like the rest of them. But we also talk, ask why, philosophize, and thereby step beyond animality, toward substance, being, reality. Or so he thinks.

But Aristotle, he's so damn serious. A deep down scientist, always at work. Apollinian head to toe. Madness, intoxication, Tuareg rock music, nowhere to be found. Yes, he drinks at dinner, but he's like Homer, for whom wine is a familiar companion but goes bad when there's too much. I'm like that most of the time. And yet, like right now, a little drunk: this feels indispensable to me. Without it I'm boxed up and meager. I need a dash now and then to let loose, recharge my batteries, keep my eyes open, fuel the winged words, tap into the stream, come to life.

(39)

Surprisingly, we managed to cobble together a fine dinner last night. It was John's birthday, and we wanted to do it right. Fresh hake. First, I threw a bunch of red and yellow peppers (industrial), doused in olive oil, into a hot oven for a few minutes. Then removed them from the pan and put in the fish, chopped olives, thyme, garlic, and some cider vinegar. Cooked it all on a high flame for another ten minutes. Put the peppers back on top. Fish was solid, light, and moist, which means I didn't ruin it by overcooking. Some brown rice, and a new item at the market: kalettes, a hybrid of brussels sprouts and kale. All they need is some oil and salt and a few minutes at a high heat. Satisfying, nutty taste. The salad was pea tendrils, watermelon radishes, carrots. Somehow it all worked. The wine was a decent Spanish white, dessert was a Sacher torte from Clear Flour, and we closed with an Alessio di Torino red vermouth, which has a strong herbal pop to it. Great to be able to eat this well in December. I get tired of white fish, though.

(40)

Friday night, which means drink some wine, and maybe, because it's cold and dark, even some whiskey. Gina and I have embraced this Semitic rhythm for decades. We need it. In the old days, we'd have some serious fun on Fridays. Now it's quieter, of course, but nonetheless it's there. I wish there were other people around. In the warm weather we're on the porch, and neighbors occasionally join in. Winter means dark alone in a warm house. Comforting, sort of, but something is missing for sure.

(41)

Some good times, some good eats. My daughters are both home for a few days during the winter holidays, and we've set the table well. The first night, Gina made a cassoulet with the pork loin from Stillman's and the white beans (heirloom) that we bought at Formaggios. A shrimp-pasta dish was my contribution on the next day. Then came the turkey dinner. Dressing made from the dry, hard bread chunks we've been stockpiling for weeks, a pile of onions and celery, chicken stock, eggs, sausage, and parsley. Mashed potatoes, made with milk, butter, cream cheese, and parm. All this produced a refrigerator full of leftovers, which we snacked on for days.

Plenty of beer and wine, and this afternoon we all played a board game. Terribly cold outside, but nice inside. The holiday lights were on, some greens hanging. Sadly we don't have a fireplace, but it almost felt like we did. Tonight I'll just make some salmon, from the Boston Smoked Fish Company, with spaghetti and pesto. And an industrial salad. More wine, no doubt. It's been nice to have some activity, some kids, in the house. Just Gina and me, it gets cramped. The first weeks of hard winter, smartly decked out for the holidays of lights, are rather pleasant. It gets harder when the lights come down, as the weeks pass by, as the routine gets old. Hope to find some good novels, for which I have a hunger these days. The newspapers, magazines, and NPR are all so terribly demoralizing. I badly need stories.

From the beginning of my study of philosophy I was dimly aware that my putative search for the Truth wasn't what it seemed. I didn't feel much like a scientist trying to crack a code. I wanted something, but wasn't sure what. Now, I might get it. I am a storyteller. Not a real truth-seeking scientist like Aristotle, who wants to understand the world as it really is. I need living, breathing stories, ones with a beginning, middle, and end. Without them, I am bereft. Which is why I go to so many movies and plays, watch hours of high-end TV, read so many novels, and have written a few myself. Even this book fits the bill. Still, it does have something to do with the truth. Doesn't it?

(42)

Fierce winter storm raging outside, but fortunately we have plenty of meat in the freezer and some supermarket vegetables in the fridge. Tonight our dinner will amount to Thanksgiving dressing. We have been collecting stale bread (mostly the sesame baguettes from Clear Flour). That plus celery, eggs, onions, chicken stock, parsley, and a couple of hot Italian sausages from Stillman's, roasted for an hour or so, will do the trick. We'll watch the snow fly horizontally and drink a bottle of Valpolicella. Gina will get a stew going today with a nice beef shank, carrots, canned tomatoes, and onions for tomorrow's dinner. After that, God willing, we should be able to get out of the house.

(43)

Salads are becoming increasingly strange in our house. Last night it was pea tendrils, shaved watermelon radish, carrots, and onions. That's about all we could find in the winter market. Not the worst, especially if sufficiently doused in olive oil and balsamic. Stillman's has plenty of meat and eggs, Brookford Farm has good cheese (cottage, cheddar), yogurt, salami, and soppressata. The fish guy from Brockton will have nice stuff at a good price, and there are potatoes. There's always fresh bread. We're not starving. Gets dark before five, and there's not much incentive to take a walk in the cold after dinner. Gina can make a great stew, and sometimes a soup, but I'm not much of a winter cook. I keep it simple, with my main tools being a grill and a timer, and if that's going to be any good, it's going to have to be fresh.

Today, though, I'm making a pea soup instead of reading Aristotle. Just sauté the onions, carrots, and celery, throw in some bacon, rinse the peas, and dump the whole mess into a pot of defrosted turkey stock. Easy. Sure, there are pots and pans, knives and bowls to wash. But easier than sitting at this table and trying to scribble something intelligent about old Aristotle.

I've been working at home recently. My own department, a place I used to enjoy, has become demoralizing. My young colleagues are hyper-professionals, top-gun types, and cold as ice. Maybe they just don't like me, but in truth, I don't think that's the problem. I cannot help them further their careers much, and so I'm just not interesting to them. Their self-absorption is not really their fault. The academic culture has molded them to be such. They do what they have to in order to survive at an ambitious research university that puts the highest premium on prestige and productivity. I'd rather stay home these days, even if that means making soup.

(44)

The pea soup was first-rate, and Gina and I ate a lot. Sadly, the amount was reduced by my having spilled a bunch of it. I was going too fast. I toweled most back into the pot, and reboiled it for cleansing purposes, and it tasted fine. As did the corn bread I made (from a mix).

(45)

So I'm supposed to be thinking about thinking—that is, working on *De Anima* III.5—but instead I'm wondering whether I should take a Stillman's pork tenderloin out of the freezer for Wednesday's dinner. I found a recipe for pork with bok choy and broccoli, which sounded like it couldn't go wrong. I don't have many ideas for dinner these days, what with nearly nothing on the farmers' shelves. But I'll have to ask Gina. We've been eating a lot of sausages lately.

I take a bagel out of the freezer for the cheese and pickled jalapeno sandwich I'll make later for lunch.

Francesco will come for dinner on Saturday. He'll bring the wine and I'll cook a brisket. This means I'll have to go to Chestnut Farm at the Boston Public

Market. Caramelized onions and parsley on top. Easy to do. Some potatoes and string beans.

(46)

Last night's dinner, to my surprise, turned out to be sort of wonderful. We got a nice thick piece of hake from Cindy. I just threw that into a very hot oven with some pickled jalapenos for fifteen minutes or so. Sprinkled some shrub, apple cider vinegar blended with cranberry and tangerine, when it came out. The rest was just stuff we had in the fridge that I had to use since we're headed out of town tomorrow. We had some big ugly potatoes, and so I peeled and mashed them. There was an old head of cabbage, so I cut it into about four thick slices, put oil and salt on, and threw them into the oven. Roasted until a little charred, and soft, and then broke it all apart and threw some vinegar on it too. I had some hen-of-the-woods (maitake) mushrooms that I had bought on Sunday at the winter market, and these I just fried up with a little oil for two minutes. And the remainder of a watermelon radish. Sliced these and put them on the plates. Comfort food. The fish was uneventful, but so fresh that it tasted good.

I've been strangely attentive to the location of small objects recently. Things in their proper places. Pens in the Chinese paintbrush holder I bought in Beijing. Postcards symmetrically positioned on the desk. Pots and pans on top of the cabinet with their handles parallel. This slight preoccupation must be an aging thing. My memory, oddly enough, seems sharper. I can see just where in the desk I had put a paper clip before I open the drawer. Some weird burst of psychic energy that comes with time shortening?

(47)

Good lord, the brisket was fabulous last night. I bought a nice one at Chestnut. Coated it with salt, paprika, cayenne, and let it sit for a few hours. Then added some red wine, garlic, bay leaves, cloves, allspice, onions. Threw it into the oven for about three hours at 325°F. (Next time, lower heat and shorter time.) Caramelized a bunch more onions, and they, with parsley, went on top just before serving. Rather nice looking, I must say. And truly delicious. Francesco brought a terrific red wine from Lebanon. I had given him a copy of Osborne's *The Wet and the Dry*, which he liked, and he had found one of the bottles Osborne had enjoyed during his visit there. Osborne liked Lebanon, or at least the parts of it that are wine friendly. Said it was what Arab culture would be like had there been no Islam.

I probably should take a few more puffs of a cigarette and return to Aristotle.

(48)

Gina and I don't feel like eating. We were both sick over the weekend, and so had to cancel a dinner party planned for Saturday night. The virus hit our stomachs, and the thought of food has become vaguely repellent. By Monday, I couldn't stand the smell of all the vegetables—beets, radishes, celery root, pea tendrils, microgreens—I had purchased. On Friday, I had made the long trek, on foot, not bike, to the Boston Public Market to get them, and the brisket from Chestnut Farm. But they're a few days old, a bit spongy, and so I threw everything out. Now the fridge is bare, and it feels better that way.

Sick, no energy, some pain. No desire for food or drink, except for sparkling water. Just sleep, and then more. Somehow, though, a balance has emerged. No activity, but no eating or smoking either, since both make me feel slightly nauseated. My system has slowed down. I've already lost a few pounds. Not the worst. Anorexia: absence of *orexis*, the Aristotelian word expressing the driving force powering all organisms. Without it, no life.

(49)

Defrosted some ground pork, made a tomato sauce, and served it with penne last night. And frozen peas. Big storm had blown in, and so our Saturday morning flight to Arizona was cancelled. We were supposed to meet our daughters in Tucson. Had a nice Airbnb lined up for the four of us, and we were looking forward to a week, my spring break, in the desert. The airline booked us another flight for Monday, so it's not yet a catastrophe, but we're stuck in the house for two more days. We tried to make the best of it last night. The wind was howling, tree branches falling, but we were at home and the food was okay, as was the bottle of Rioja. Still, can't say I'm feeling particularly cheerful.

I'm thinking about calling it quits as a professor. Almost everything at the university demoralizes me. I still get a small charge from the teaching, but the students are not enough to get me through the day without pain. My colleagues repel me, as does the administration and its many bogus initiatives, all of which are designed to increase the prestige of Boston University and give it a larger market share. I have no idea what I would do instead. I'll probably keep writing, but at some point I'll have to face the fact that I wrote a bunch of books and yet the world did not change. Plus, I can't write more than two or three hours a day. But this chapter is coming to a close, and maybe I should bolt before my spirits deteriorate even further. Maybe spend long stretches of time in Italy?

A cartoon from the *New Yorker*: a tombstone in a graveyard. On it are the words, "All that kale for nothing."

(50)

The cookie the flight attendant gave us wasn't bad, nor was the cheese and pickled jalapeno sandwich with mayo and mustard on an Iggy's poppy seed bagel that I had brought. Flying to Phoenix after a two-day delay. The plane, like the previous two or three we've taken, has been exceptionally quiet. Everyone is plugged into a screen and has headphones on. Me too. I watched a nice movie, *Me and Earl and the Dying Girl*, which I've seen before. So many movies, TV shows, stories with beginnings, middles, and ends, tight little wholes to transport me out of the indefinite grind. For a little while. I need them. Badly.

For just this reason, then, Plato (as author of the Socrates stories), not Aristotle, as the hero of my book?

(51)

Nothing in the fridge, and not much to look forward to either. The winter farmers' markets have closed. The farmers have nothing left in storage—not even beets or turnips or carrots—and the fields are still crusty with ice and snow. The only options these days are industrial. The asparagus from Peru is okay, as is the broccolini from who knows where. We can still buy excellent beef, pork, fish, and poultry at the Boston Public Market. There's also fresh pasta, good cheese, and even some jars of tomato sauce, which taste fine. But pretty dull, especially compared to what's coming in a few months. But no fresh fruit or vegetables on the shelves yet, and so we just have to wait. These are the days when we often go to restaurants. Since Lineage closed, however, none of them, even those whose food is good, are particularly nourishing.

I wish I had a larger group of friends, with whom I could drink bottles of wine, talk, and laugh. But I don't. The ones I've known longest are getting old and tired. Plus, most of them don't like to cook or give parties. I love doing both, but just can't continue to muster the energy to be, yet again, the master of ceremonies. Nor can I bring myself to drink alone.

Fixed on my screen, I keep cranking this shit out, and who knows why.

And yet: today, late March, the sun is shining and I'm thinking about bringing my bike out from the basement. I'll pump the tires, clean the chain, and, who knows, maybe soon I'll ride down the esplanade on the Charles River and see what I can find. Maybe those delicious crab cakes at Red's Seafood Market?

(52)

Store-bought pesto, Barilla thick spaghetti, smoked salmon from Boston Smoked Fish, and industrial arugula. That with a glass of red wine, and it was a pretty good meal. The best to be expected at this dreary time of year. Threw a bit of a bash a few days ago. Had a friend visiting from Germany. Her husband, a marvelous man, died a year ago. A gorgeous beef tenderloin from Chestnut Farms, mashed potatoes (garlic, cream cheese, parmigiana, milk, and lots of kosher salt), and a salad. Don't really like beef tenderloin much. Unlike a ribeye thrown on a hot grill, with only salt and pepper, it need supplementation. So I made a sauce. Crème fraiche, orange zest, and horseradish. I don't go for sauces, and I'm not much of a cream guy, so I wasn't crazy about any of this, but my guests seemed to like it. Gina made an almond meal, olive oil cake. Topped with Fiasco gelato, it was delicious. It may be dark, but we did all right. Two or three bottles of wine helped. Got us through another night with a few laughs.

(53)

Gina made a lovely lamb stew last night. Meat from Chestnut Farms, very tender. Lots of spices, chick peas, raisins, couscous. Broccoli and carrots on the side. Even though it is nearly mid-May, the air was cool, and so it hit the spot.

Suffering from another shoulder injury. Who knows what caused it. Swimming, most likely, with my terribly bad stroke. I had a similar problem a couple of years ago in my right shoulder, but a training regimen suggested by a physical therapist seemed to work pretty well, and I'd been feeling good, and so, naturally, I started to swim more frequently and with a bit more vigor. Now I'm paying the price. I feel somewhat bereft. I've been working my shoulders for two years, and now my left one hurts more than the right one ever did. Add that to an arthritic knee and hip, and I'm creaking. Wearing out. Maybe already worn.

It's supposed to be sunny on Friday, which is opening day at the Copley Farmers Market. So Gina and I plan to ride down there in the afternoon, pick up whatever they have, and serve it to some friends. We might even be able to eat on the back deck, if it stays warm after the sun goes down. The friends are all graduate students. In other words, young, and so not friends in the truest sense. Still, we like them, and we much appreciate being around people who do not talk about knee and hip replacements. No organ recitals on Friday night, no discussions of retirement scenarios. Just good food—I'm thinking steak, of course—plenty to drink, some laughs. A great gift from my profession. Being able to hang out with people in their twenties.

(54)

Dinner was first-rate last night. I gave up on the steak idea, and went with scallops, bought from Red's, and a salad of arugula and microgreens from Siena Farms. Fresh pasta from Valenti's. Tomatoes came from a can, but at least they were San Marzano, peeled and flavorful. Dessert from Clear Flour. The same Valpolicella we enjoyed with Francesco. As hoped, our young guests were a pleasure. The asparagus wasn't as good as it was last year, though. The spring has been cold.

Notes

1 The Eatingest Epic

1   All citations in this chapter are from *The Odyssey of Homer*, translated by Robert Fitzgerald (New York: Random House, 1990). Fitzgerald's version of this famous book, from his word choice to his spelling of names to his line numbering, is idiosyncratic. But it reads extremely well. For a less imaginative, more literal translation, consult Richmond Lattimore's *The Odyssey of Homer* (New York: Harper, 2007).

    I would like to thank Rob Tempio, who suggested the title of this book to me.

2   Actually, his first stop is to visit Nestor in Pylos.

3   Aristotle, *Poetics*, 6. Translated by Stephen Halliwell (Chapel Hill: University of North Carolina Press, 1987), p. 55.

4   Fitzgerald renders the hero's name as "Akhilleus," but I retain the more familiar "Achilles" when I am not quoting directly from the text.

5   Achilles, however, is confused. His very next statement is to wish for his son to win the same sort of glory as did his father.

2 Dionysus

1   The text is William Arrowsmith's translation in *Eurpides V*, edited by David Grene and Richmond Lattimore (Chicago: University of Chicago Press, 1968).

2   E. R. Dodds, *Euripides Bacchae* (Oxford: Clarendon Press, 1983), p. xii.

3   Lawrence Osborne, *The Wet and the Dry: A Drinker's Journey* (New York: Crown, 2013), p. 67.

4   Osborne, *The Wet and the Dry*, p. 141. Hereafter, in quoting from this book, I will simply place the page number in parentheses.

5   William James, *Varieties of Religious Experience* (Oxford: Oxford University Press, 2012). Hereafter, in quoting from this book, I will simply place the page numbers in parentheses.

6   Friedrich Nietzsche, *The Birth of Tragedy*, translated by Walter Kaufmann (New York: Vintage Books, 1967). Hereafter, in quoting from this book, I will simply place the page number in parentheses.

7   This line appears in Sophocles' play, *Oedipus at Colonus*, 1224.

8 Friedrich Nietzsche, *Philosophy in the Tragic Age of the Greeks*, translated by
   Marianne Cowan (Chicago: Regnery Gateway, 1962), p. 52.
9 These comments about Nietzsche were first formulated in my book, *Thinking
   Philosophically* (Oxford: Wiley, 2016), p. 199.

Interlude

1 For information on James's use of nitrous oxide, see Dmitri Tymoczko, "The
   Nitrous Oxide Philosopher," *Atlantic Monthly*, Vol. 277.5, May 1996, pp. 93–101.

3 Socrates

1 Friedrich Nietzsche, *The Birth of Tragedy*, translated by Walter Kaufmann
   (New York: Vintage Books, 1967), p. 86. Hereafter, in quoting from this book, I will
   simply place the page number in parentheses.
2 The translations of Plato's *Symposium* are my own. The Greek text is J. Burnet's
   (Oxford: Oxford University Press, 1964). I will not address the question of whether
   the Socrates who appears in Plato's dialogue resembles the historical figure or
   whether he functions as Plato's mouthpiece to express his own views. These are
   honorable questions, but in this book they are not mine.
3 Plato here has Socrates shift to the voice of (to imitate) the priestess Diotima.
   Nonetheless, since it is Socrates who is actually doing the talking, I will use either
   "he" or "Socrates" to refer to the speaker.
4 Who this guide is, is never said. Perhaps it is Eros himself; perhaps it is an older
   philosopher.
5 Friedrich Nietzsche, *Philosophy in the Tragic Age of the Greeks*, translated by
   Marianne Cowan (Chicago: Regnery Gateway, 1962), p. 52.
6 Explaining how particulars "participate" in universals, or, more generally, what the
   relationship is between them, becomes the task of a vast chunk of the subsequent
   history of Western philosophy.
7 My statement that for Plato the sensible world is "no more than a fleeting image of
   a higher, more substantial and permanent reality" ultimately requires a great deal of
   elaboration. In fact, Plato does not simply relegate sensible beings to an inferior level
   of reality. In other words, he does not straightforwardly endorse what scholars call a
   "two-world" theory of reality, in which the sensible and the intelligible domains are
   radically separate. Instead, his is an account rich in nuance and complexity. This also
   applies to his comments about food and drink. While they are indeed frequently
   dismissive, Plato understands and takes seriously their counterpoint. The present

chapter should thus be taken, above all else, as an invitation to readers to study the dialogues on their own, and even to challenge the views presented here.

8   It must be noted that Plato, the author of the dialogues, is not simply equivalent to Socrates, who is their hero. While Socrates does indeed profess a wholehearted commitment to rational argument alone, Plato wrote beautiful crafted works that, in addition to being philosophically rich, are literary masterpieces. As such, even if his Socrates (in *Republic* Book II, for example) may seem to be the single-minded critic of Homer and the other poets, Plato himself is a far more complicated, more mixed, proposition.

9   Aristotle, *The Poetics*, ch. 22, translated by Stephen Halliwell (Chapel Hill: University of North Carolina Press, 1987), p. 55.

10 Consider *Phaedrus* 248b, where the human soul is said to be "nourished" on the plain of Truth.

11 This passage clearly refers to the famous "allegory of the cave," which opens Book VII of the *Republic*.

12 In fairness, Alcibiades does say that, despite the fact that Socrates could go long stretches without bothering to eat or drink, he also "could really enjoy a good feast" (*Symposium*, 220a). This is precisely the sort of tension referred to in note 8.

13 The translations of Plato's *Phaedo* are my own. The Greek text is J. Burnet's (Oxford: Oxford University Press, 1967).

14 Nietzsche is actually talking about Christianity here, but its applicability to Socrates will become apparent shortly.

15 This well-known phrase comes from the preface to Friedrich Nietzsche, *Beyond Good and Evil*, translated by Walter Kaufman (New York: Vintage, 1989), p. 14.

16 Saint Augustine, *City of God*, translated by Henry Bettenson (New York: Penguin, 2003), XXII.24.

17 Saint Augustine, *Confessions*, translated by F. J. Sheed (Indianapolis: Hackett, 1993).

18 https://www.soylent.com/; website as of March 24, 2018.

19 Max Weber, *The Protestant Ethics and the Spirit of Capitalism*, translated by Stephen Kalberg (New York: Oxford University Press, 2011).

4 Aristotle

1   Saint Augustine, *City of God*, translated by Henry Bettenson (New York: Penguin, 2003), XXII.24.

2   The translations of Aristotle's *Physics* are my own. The Greek text is W. D. Ross's (Oxford: Oxford University Press, 1950).

3   The Greek word *phuein*, which means "to grow," is the root of *phusis*. The word can also mean "give birth to."

4   William James, *Varieties of Religious Experience* (Oxford: Oxford University Press, 2012), p. 48.

5   Aristotle does think religion is important, but in only one limited domain: the political. By his lights, religious beliefs can help keep uneducated people in line. See *Metaphysics*, 1074b1–7. Also, see *Politics*, 1322b18–20, where Aristotle explains the strictly administrative role that priests should play in the city. By his lights, beyond its civic function, religion offers nothing nourishing to the human spirit.

6   The translations of Aristotle's *Metaphysics* are my own. The Greek text is Werner Jaeger's (Oxford: Oxford University Press, 1957).

7   Translations of *De Anima* are my own. The Greek text is W. D. Ross's (Oxford: Oxford University Press, 1963).

8   Leon Kass, *The Hungry Soul* (Chicago: University of Chicago Press, 1999), p. 23.

9   In the cases of seeing, smelling, and hearing, the medium is obvious. Touch and taste are more complicated.

10 These diagrams, and the thoughts behind them, were originally used in my book *Retrieving the Ancients* (Oxford: Blackwell, 2004). They were then recycled in *Retrieving Aristotle in an Age of Crisis* (Albany: SUNY Press, 2013). And now they are here.

11 This passage comes from Galileo's book *The Assayer*. Translated by Stephen Halliwell (Chapel Hill: University of North Carolina Press, 1987), p. 55. I also discussed this passage in *Retrieving the Ancients*, p. 54.

12 The translations of Aristotle's *Nicomachean Ethics* are my own. The Greek text is Ingram Bywater's (Oxford: Oxford University Press, 1965).

13 An obvious question that should be directed at this argument is, is Aristotle illicitly inferring from what is true of the parts to what is true of the whole?

14 Aristotle himself does not use the phrase "active intellect," but it has long been associated with him.

15 Scholars have debated Aristotle's teaching about *nous* for millennia.

16 Aristotle's *Posterior Analytics*, I.18, translated by Hugh Tredennick (Cambridge, MA: Harvard University Press, 1976).

Bibliography

Aristotle. *De Anima*. Edited by W. D. Ross (Oxford: Oxford University Press, 1967).

Aristotle. *The Metaphysics*. Edited by Werner Jaeger (Oxford: Oxford University Press, 1957).

Aristotle. *The Nicomachean Ethics*. Edited by Ingram Bywater (Oxford: Oxford University Press, 1965).

Aristotle. *The Physics*. Edited by W. D. Ross (Oxford: Oxford University Press, 1950).

Aristotle. *Posterior Analytics*. Translated by G. P. Goold (Cambridge, MA: Harvard University Press, 1976).

Aristotle. *The Poetics*. Translated by Stephen Halliwell (Chapel Hill: University of North Carolina Press, 1987).

Augustine. *The City of God*. Translated by Henry Bettenson (New York: Penguin, 2003).

Augustine. *Confessions*. Translated by F. J. Sheed (Indianapolis: Hackett, 1993).

Euripides. *Bacchae*. Translated by William Arrowsmith. In *Euripides* V, edited by David Grene and Richmond Lattimore (Chicago: University of Chicago Press, 1968).

Dodds, E. R. *Euripides Bacchae* (Oxford: Clarendon Press, 1983).

Halliwell, Stephen (translator). *Aristotle's Poetics* (Chapel Hill: University of North Carolina Press, 1987).

Homer. *The Odyssey*. Translated by Robert Fitzgerald (New York: Random House, 1990).

Kass, Leon. *The Hungry Soul* (Chicago: University of Chicago Press, 1999).

Nietzsche, Friedrich. *The Birth of Tragedy*. Translated by Walter Kaufmann (New York: Vintage Books, 1967).

Nietzsche, Friedrich. *Philosophy in the Tragic Age of the Greeks*. Translated by Marianne Cowan (Chicago: Regnery Gateway, 1962).

Osborne, Lawrence. *The Wet and the Dry: A Drinker's Journey* (New York: Crown, 2013).

Plato. *Phaedo*. Edited by J. Burnet (Oxford: Oxford University Press, 1967).

Plato. *Symposium*. Edited by J. Burnet (Oxford: Oxford University Press, 1964).

Roochnik, David. *Thinking Philosophically* (Oxford: Wiley, 2016).

Tymoczko, Dmitri. "The Nitrous Oxide Philosopher." *Atlantic Monthly*, Vol. 277.5, May 1996, pp. 93–101.

Weber, Max. *The Protestant Ethics and the Spirit of Capitalism*. Translated by Stephen Kalberg (New York: Oxford University Press, 2011).

Index

Achilles 14, 29–30, 68, 69–70, 163 nn.4, 5
activity 127, 140
actuality (*energeia, entelecheia*) 122–3,
    127, 133, 140
Aeschylus 72, 118
Agamemnon 2, 17
Agathon 79, 80
Alcibiades 86–8
alcohol 49, 53, 59–61, 63–6, 86, 88
analogy 88, 126–8, 133
Andromache 68
animals (*zôa*)
    and Aristotle's zoology 120–1, 123–4,
        136, 137–8, 139–40, 149–50
    humans as 35–6, 126–7, 133, 136,
        141–3, 146–7, 150–1
    as wholes 28, 130–3
Antiphon 122
Aphrodite 49–50
Apollinian 66–8, 70, 72–4, 118, 124–7, 154
Apollo 66–70
a priori knowledge 93–4
Archilochus 72
Aristotle 10–11, 88, 120–51, 154, 156
    De Anima 127–34, 137, 143–6, 150–1
    The Generation of Animals 137–8
    The Metaphysics 121, 125–6, 146–9,
        166 n.5
    Nicomachean Ethics 138, 141–2,
        150–1
    The Physics 120–3
    Poetics 10–11, 124
    Politics 140, 165 n. 5
    Posterior Analytics 148
Argo 22
Athena 8, 12, 18–19, 27, 31, 35
Athens 79, 90
Augustine, St. 95–101, 103, 117–18

beautiful (*kalon*) 68–9, 80, 82, 83–6, 95
    (*see also* of Beauty *under* form)
becoming 71, 83

being (*to on*) 90, 96, 99, 118, 120, 130–1
    ontology 121, 124
Bildungsroman 82
birth 46, 81–2, 93
body (*soma*) 7, 82–3, 90–1, 100–1,
    127–32

Cadmus 46–7, 50, 58
Calvin, John 101–3, 117
chorus 72–4
Christianity 94–103, 165 n.14
conversation 11, 84, 88–9

dance 50, 64, 74, 75
Dante 28, 30
Darwin, Charles 120, 138
death 3, 6, 69, 90–4, 95
    as constitutive of human life 3, 6
    life after 28–30, 90–4, 101
    and philosophy 91, 95–6, 143
    self–sacrifice 137–8
deficiency 92–3
deus ex machina 35
Dionysian
    and intoxication 49, 51, 58, 60, 64, 66,
        75, 79, 88, 153
    James as 61, 63, 65–6
    resistance to 46, 53, 58–61 (*see also*
        Pentheus)
        Aristotle as anti–Dionysian 124–5,
        126, 154
    and Silenus 68–70
    and Socrates 79, 88
    and tragedy 72–4, 79,
Dionysus 65–6, 68, 72, 76, 79, 87
    in Euripides' *Bacchae* 46–58
    and intoxication 49, 51, 58, 64, 153
    the god 46, 60–1, 64–5, 66, 68, 72
Diotima 80, 137, 164
divine 5, 14, 61, 137–8, 141–3, 150–1
DNA 81, 123
Dodds, E. R. 48

dreams 25–7, 28–9, 67–8
drugs 9–10, 75, 147
drunkeness
    consequences from 18, 45–6, 58
    as part of human life 59, 63–4, 99, 154
    in Plato 86–7

Egypt 3, 60
Eidothea (*divine form*) 3–5
empiricism 94, 146–50
end (*telos*) 124, 131, 138–43
energy 7, 35–6, 93, 129, 131
equal *see* of Equality *under* form
eros (love) 79–86, 137–8, 164 n.4
eternal 28, 94–100, 103, 117, 136, 138, 146
Euripides 61, 65, 72
    Bacchae 46–58, 70, 72–3, 87, 142
experience (*empeiria*) 5, 93, 126, 146–50
    mystical experiences 61–5, 71, 73, 75–6,
        99, 125

fermentation 49, 53, 64
Fielding, Henry 3
flux 31, 36, 68, 70, 83, 85–6
    Protean 12, 16, 27, 53, 119
form (*eidos*) 117–19
    of Beauty 83, 85, 87, 119
    eidos 3–4, 121–4, 126, 138
    of Equality 92–4, 124
    essence 71
    in Homer 3–7, 11, 12, 27, 36, 66, 68, 74
    intelligible 71, 83, 89–90, 91–4, 96,
        145, 150–1
    maintaining 7, 12, 36, 66, 74, 118, 128,
        130–2, 138
    sensible 133–4, 126, 144
    as species 121–4, 127, 151
Franklin, Benjamin 103
function 4, 128, 131–2, 135, 139–40
future *see under* time

Galileo 135–6
God 61, 63, 94–103, 117–18
gods 5–6, 46–7, 51–3, 69–70, 142
guest code 1–2, 17, 20, 31, 33

Hades 23, 28–30, 70, 86, 120
happiness, (*eudaimonia*) 81, 138,
        140–1, 150–1
health 80, 89

Hektor 68
Helen 9–10, 36, 62
Hera 46
Heraclitus 71
Homer 66, 96, 100–1, 117–18
    Iliad 14, 43, 68
    Odyssey 43, 66
        Book IV, 1–9, 31
        Book V, 12
        Book VI, 12–14
        Book VIII, 68
        Book IX, 14–18, 21, 119–20
        Book X, 45
        Book XI, 23, 28–30, 69–70
        Book XII, 20
        Book XIII, 18–19
        Book XIV, 31, 33–4, 45–6
        Book XVI, 22
        Book XVII, 22, 31–2
        Book XVIII, 9–10, 30, 32
        Book XIX, 22, 24–6
        Book XX, 26
        Book XXI, 45
        Book XXII, 32–3
        Book XXIII, 23–4, 26–7
        Book XXIV, 19–20, 34
human finitude *see* transience
hunger 89
hylomorphism 122

image (*eidolon, eidola*) 28–30, 67–8, 86,
        164 n.7
immortality
    of gods 5–6
    metaphorical 30, 81, 87–8
    rejection of 6, 16
    of the soul 91–94, 143–6, 150
    striving for 137–8, 142–3
individuation 68, 119, 124, 125
induction 147–8
infinite 97, 139–40
intellect (*nous*) 86, 91, 141–2, 143–6, 150–1
intelligible objects (*noêta*) 144–5
intoxication *see under* Dionysian
Islam 59
Ithaka 7–8, 18, 20–3, 33–5

James, William 61–6, 125, 71, 75–6,
        88, 125
justice 30–5

Kalypso 6–7, 12, 14, 100
Kass, Leon 129–33
knowledge 84, 93–4, 125–6, 146–50
    (*see also* self–knowledge)
Kyklops *see* Polyphemus

Laërtês 19–20
Lakedaimon 2, 7
language 63–4, 70–2, 82–3, 119, 122–3,
    125 (*see also* logos)
laughter 18, 51
Lebanon 60, 158–9
logos (speech, language, reasoning,
    thought)
    animal with 140–1, 143, 147, 150,
      151, 154
    as "explanation" or "theory" 121, 124,
      134–5, 146, 149–50
    as "language" or "speech" 82–3,
      88–90, 119
Lotus Eaters 16–17
lying 18–20

Maenads 47–8, 50, 53–4, 56–7, 73
materialism 122–3, 129, 132
matter 36, 121–4, 127, 133, 138
measurement 92, 97
memory 11–12, 25–7, 36, 120, 146, 148–9
Meneláos 1–5, 7–10, 12, 31, 81, 103
mercy 32
metabolism (*metabolê*) 35–6, 96, 131
metaphor 30, 81, 87–9, 95, 117, 124–5,
    137, 151
moral 30–3, 118
mortality *see* transience
music 64–5, 70–3, 70, 118, 126
muthos (myth, plot, story) 10, 124 (*see also*
    stories)
mystical experience *see under* experience

nature, natural 54, 95, 120–4, 126–7
Nausikaa 12–14, 31
Nietzsche
    on Christianity 96–7, 165 n.14
    on Homer 66–8
    on music 70–2
    on Socrates 79, 83, 87, 88, 93–4, 136
    on tragedy 72–4, 118
nothingness 36, 62, 70, 74
nouns 122

nourishing 129–33, 136, 138, 144
nutrition 127–33, 138, 140, 143, 144

Odysseus 2–36, 45, 66–70, 100,
    117, 120
Olympian gods 5, 69–70
orexis (urge, drive) 138, 159
Osborne, Lawrence 49, 53, 58–61,
    64, 158–9

Pakistan 59, 60
particulars 83–6, 94, 96, 119, 147–8,
    164 n.6
Penelope 6–7, 23–30, 35, 66–7
Pentheus 47, 49–56, 60–1, 142
perception 133–6, 140, 144, 146–9
Phaiákians 12, 15–16, 18
philosophy 81, 86–8, 91
Plato 164 nn.2, 3, 165 n.8
    as Aristotle's teacher 121, 124, 127,
      138, 160
    Phaedo 90–4, 120–1, 127, 143, 150
    Phaedrus 87, 165 n.10
    Republic 88, 165 n.8
    Symposium 79–87, 137, 143, 150
Platonism 95, 165 n.8
pleasure 89–90, 126
Polemarchus 88
Polyphêmos 17–18, 20–1, 27, 32
Poseidon 12, 17, 21, 23, 27
potentiality 122–3, 127–30, 133–4,
    135, 144–6
predestination 101–2
pregnancy *see* sexual reproduction
Protestantism 101–3
Proteus 3–5, 12
psuchê (soul, life force)
    as the breathe of life 28–30, 119
    on the immortality of it 93–4,
      120, 143–6
    as opposed to the body 83, 89, 90–1
    as a principle or cause 121, 124, 127–9,
      131–3, 133–8, 139–41
purification (*katharsis*) 91

realism 72, 135
recognition 21, 22–7, 47, 57
recollection 90–4
religion 61–2, 64, 75, 125, 166 n.5
retribution 30–5

Saudi Arabia 59–60
self–knowledge 51, 53, 61
self–nourishment 129–32, 134, 136,
    137, 145
Semele 46–7
sexual repression 49–52, 60
sexual reproduction 81, 87, 123, 137,
    143, 151
shades 28–30, 69, 120
Silenus see under *Dionysian*
simile 13, 28, 67–8
Sirens 20
Socrates 79–103, 117–20, 121, 137–8,
    143, 150–1
    and metaphors 81, 86–9, 95, 100,
        124, 137
    as Plato's character 160, 164 nn.2, 3,
        165 n.8
Sophocles 72, 163 n.7
soul see *psuchê*
Soylent 100–1, 103
species 121–7, 138, 140, 143, 149
stories 10–21, 27, 62, 74, 120, 160
    storytelling 30, 36, 66, 156
substance (*ousia*) 62, 121, 127

Teirêsias 23–4, 27, 51–2
Telémakhos 2, 5, 7–10, 22
Thebes 46
theoretical activity 141–2, 146–51
thinking 91, 141, 144–6
time 7, 27, 70, 96–100, 103
    future 11–12, 36, 80–1, 96–7,
        118, 137–8
    present 11, 70, 98–9, 118
tragedy 56, 72–4, 79, 118

transience *see also* flux, time, immortality
    celebrating it 16, 36
    distraction from 10, 12
    and eating 3–9, 33–4
    as a theme of this book 118–19
Trojan War 1–36, 62, 68
truth
    and fiction 12, 18, 119
    horrifying 58
    mystical 63–4
    philosophical 86–7, 91, 124, 136
    scientific 148, 150, 156

universal
    above the particulars 82–6, 87,
        90–1, 119
    in the particular 124, 147–50

vanity 62
virtue (*aretê*) 140–2

Weber, Max 101–3
whole 10–12, 124, 128, 129–32, 139
wine
    comforts of 9–10, 51, 62, 65
    with dinner 2–3, 36, 66, 118, 151
    god of wine *see* Dionysus
    as a metaphor 79, 87–90
    negatives of 45–6
    and tragedy 72–4

Zeus
    father of Athena 12
    father of Dionysus 46
    god of guest friendship 1, 17, 33–4
    versus mortal men 5, 9, 81, 97